Fallen Angels

By Ken Johnson, Th.D.

Fallen Angels
by Ken Johnson, Th.D.

Printed in the United States of America

ISBN 148490558X
EAN-13 978-1484905586

Unless otherwise indicated, Bible quotations are taken
from the King James Version.

Contents

Introduction

This book on the Fallen Angels is compiled from the King James Bible, Talmud, Mishna, and midrashim of the Jews, including the *Ancient Book of Jasher*. It also includes information from Jewish messianic festivals and Dead Sea Scrolls, like the books of *Jubilees* and *Enoch*, and information from the ancient church fathers on angels, demons, Nephilim, and other spirits.

Many other authors who have attempted to create a dictionary of angels have also included medieval resources like the Kabala and Islamic texts. I have opted to ignore any text that is not at least two thousand years old. I have included a minority of Gnostic elements as given from the ancient church fathers.

This book can be a companion guide to *Ancient Paganism*.

Fallen Angels

Creation of Angels

Classes of Angels

The word used in the Bible for angel really means "messenger." Sometimes God sent a human messenger, like a prophet, to speak to someone. Most of the time in the Bible, the messenger is a non-human creature. God created these non-human messengers before humans (Job 38:4-7). Today, Christians refer to them as angels. Rabbinic legend tells us there are ten different types of angels. Biblically we know of at least four classes: cherubim, seraphim, angels, and archangels.

The Bible does not say exactly when or where the angels were created or how they exist. We do know that the angels were already in existence and Lucifer had already fallen when Adam was in the Garden of Eden.

General Characteristics

We know a lot about angels from Scripture. They are innumerable (Heb. 12:22) spirit beings (Heb. 1:14) who are normally invisible (2 Kings 6:15-17), but can materialize in human form (Gen. 18:2-8). They were created by God (Ps. 148:2, 5) but are not gods. They are a higher life form than man (Heb. 2:7), are powerful (Ps. 103:20), are organized into orders (Isa. 6:2), and eat manna as food (Psalm 78:25). They can be princes over nations (Dan. 12:1) and may use flaming swords (Gen. 3:24).

Fallen Angels

What are They like?

Angels are immortal (Luke 20:36), holy (Matt. 25:31), wise (2 Sam 14:17, 20), meek (Jude 9), and obedient to God (Ps. 103:20). They possess emotions (Luke 15:10). Obedient angels remain unmarried in heaven (Matt. 22:30) but some fallen angels left heaven and procreated with humans (Genesis 6:4). Angels do not create anything (John 1:1-3) and are not perfect (Job 4:18). They care about human things (1 Pet. 1:12). They know who are true Christians (Matt. 13:24-30, 39) and Christians will judge them (1 Cor. 6:3).

What are Their Abilities?

Angels have some amazing abilities. They can heal people (John 5:4), but they can also blind (Gen. 19:10, 11), mute (Luke 1:20), and kill (Isa. 37:36). In fact there was a time when one angel destroyed an entire army of 185,000 warriors in one night (2 Kings 19:35)! They have rescued people from prison (Acts 12:5-11).

What are Their Duties?

Angels protected the Messiah while He was on earth (Psalm 91:11-12), and worship Him (Heb. 1:6). They do not wish to be bowed down to (Rev. 19:7-10) or be worshiped (Rev. 22:8-9). Angels rejoice over sinners who repent and become true Christians (Luke 15:10). They warn of judgment (Gen 19:1, 13) and will pour out judgment on earth (Rev. 4-19).

Angels obviously have free will or none of them would have fallen. We also understand that since angels are a separate creation of God, men do not become angels after death.

Angels and Archangels

The Bible teaches angels and archangels look very much like men. The angel Gabriel looked so much like a human being that Scripture sometimes calls him a man (Daniel 9:21). They obviously don't die because Gabriel revealed a prophecy to Daniel in 536 BC and announced the birth of Jesus to Mary about 2 BC!

Among the angels there are ranks. Some are referred to as princes and others as chief princes (Daniel 10:13). The exact meaning of these titles remains obscure.

Guardian Angels

The guardian angel is one who protects a Christian, or some special person God wants protected. We see many instances in Scripture where this occurs. Jesus mentions the "little ones" are protected by angels. In Acts 12, Peter's angel broke him out of jail; so the apostles were protected by them as well.

> "Take heed that ye despise not one of these little ones; for I say unto you, that in heaven their angels do always behold the face of My Father which is in heaven." *Matthew 18:10*

> "And they said unto her, Thou art mad. But she constantly affirmed that it was even so. Then said they, It is his angel. But Peter continued

knocking: and when they had opened *the door*, and saw him, they were astonished."
Acts 12:15-16

Death Angels

Angels are incredibly powerful beings. Most people today have no idea what an angel is really capable of. In the book of Isaiah there was an Assyrian army consisting of 185,000 seasoned warriors. They had besieged the city of Jerusalem; so God ordered an angel to intervene. In one night that *one* angel killed every single one of the 185,000 Assyrians!

> "Then the angel of the LORD went forth, and smote in the camp of the Assyrians a hundred and fourscore and five thousand: and when they arose early in the morning, behold, they were all dead corpses." *Isaiah 37:36*

Exodus 12:23 describes how God passed over the Egyptians and killed their firstborn during the tenth plague. The Rabbis taught God did this through a destroying angel.

Paul mentions this "destroyer" in 1 Corinthians 10:10. Paul is referring to the event recorded in Numbers 14:37, where the destroyer (plague in KJV) killed the ten spies who murmured about entering the Promised Land. The Hebrew word used here is *magpah*. It is an unusual word for plague. In the Bible we only see it here, in the death of the firstborn in Egypt, and in the plague that Phinehas stopped in Numbers 25:7, 8. In other Jewish texts, the word is also used for the event where the angel slew the 185,000 Assyrians.

In Modern Hebrew the word *magpah* means a "stroke." So when an angel kills someone, it appears to be a stroke, brain hemorrhage, brain lesion, or an aneurism. This does not mean that everyone who has a stroke is killed by an angel.

Notice the parallels. The ten faithless spies wanted to give up the Promised Land; the Egyptians wanted to keep the Israelis from leaving Egypt and entering the Promised Land; and the Assyrians wanted to displace the Israelites out of the Promised Land. Each group was destroyed by angelic strokes. Remember that Ariel Sharon gave up the Gaza strip and within a year's time suffered a stroke!

Seraphim

The word *seraph* is a Hebrew word. When used as a noun it usually refers to fiery or poisonous serpents. As a verb it means "burning." Using the base word *seraph* leads us to believe that the seraphim are either aflame themselves or serpent-like or both.

Isaiah gave us a description of the seraphim angels. These fiery serpent-like seraphim are creatures with six wings (three pairs).

"In the year that king Uzziah died I saw also the Lord sitting upon a throne, high and lifted up, and his train filled the temple. Above it stood the seraphim: each one had six wings; with twain he covered his face, and with twain he covered his feet, and with twain he did fly. And one cried unto another, and said, Holy, holy, holy, *is* the LORD of hosts: the whole earth *is* full of his glory." *Isaiah 6:1-3*

Cherubim

Today most of the cherub pictures and statues we see are made in the image of a baby human with little wings. This is not the biblical cherub.

The prophet Ezekiel had visions of cherubim in wheels around God's throne. Notice how he describes them from these two passages. The four faces are the same except Ezekiel 10 replaces the face of the ox with the face of a cherub.

"As for the likeness of their faces, they four had the face of a man, and the face of a lion, on the right side: and they four had the face of an <u>ox</u> on the left side; they four also had the face of an eagle." *Ezekiel 1:10*

"And every one had four faces: the first face *was* the face of a cherub, and the second face *was* the face of a man, and the third the face of a lion, and the fourth the face of an eagle." *Ezekiel 10:14*

One can see the face of a cherub looks like the face of an ox or a bull. This might be what the legend of the Minotaur is based upon.

Ezekiel tells us that cherubim have four wings (two pairs) with the basic form of a man, with the exception of cloven hoofs instead of feet. Their heads look much more like a bull's than a human's.

In Genesis we know cherubim were placed at the entrance to the Garden of Eden after the fall of man to prevent Adam from re-entering the garden. This cherub had a special weapon.

> "So he drove out the man; and he placed at the east of the garden of Eden Cherubims, and a flaming sword which turned every way, to keep the way of the tree of life." *Genesis 3:24*

We also see decorative cherubim placed in the tabernacle on and around the mercy seat. Some scholars think these passages indicate cherubim are normally guardians of places and objects.

> "[2]Be not forgetful to entertain strangers: for thereby some have entertained angels unawares." *Hebrews 13:2*

Where Did the Fallen Angels Come From?
Originally all the angels served and worshiped God, their Creator. They were curious about the things God was

creating and even curious about mankind. No angel is all-knowing. The holy angels still desire to figure out the prophecies given in the Scriptures of old.

> "Concerning this salvation, the prophets, who spoke of the grace that was to come to you, searched intently and with the greatest care, trying to find out the time and circumstances to which the Spirit of Christ in them was pointing when he predicted the sufferings of Christ and the glories that would follow. It was revealed to them that they were not serving themselves but you, when they spoke of the things that have now been told you by those who have preached the gospel to you by the Holy Spirit sent from heaven. Even angels long to look into these things."
> *1 Peter 1:10-12 NIV*

When Lucifer rebelled, he deceived one third of the angels into following him. He may have suggested God was not telling the truth about Himself and creation.

Angels are sometimes referred to as "stars." This may mean they shine brightly, like stars.

> "And his tail drew the third part of the stars of heaven... And the great dragon was cast out, that old serpent, called the Devil, and Satan, which deceiveth the whole world: he was cast out into the earth, and his angels were cast out with him."
> *Revelation 12:4, 9*

The Bible tells us that fallen angels differ from holy angels. These angels fell through pride (1 Tim. 3:6). God prepared hell for fallen angels (Matt. 25:41). Some fallen angels are already imprisoned (2 Pet. 2:4; Jude 6), but others are free and will make war on the saints in the last days (Rev. 12:7-17).

The ancient church fathers give us more confirmation about what has been discussed so far. They agree that Lucifer spoke though the serpent in the Garden of Eden, and that only fallen angels desire to be worshiped as gods.

"This Eve, became the author of sin, when in the beginning, she was deceived by the serpent. That wicked demon, who also is called Satan, who then spoke to her through the serpent" *Theophilus 2.28*

"...nor do the angels, inasmuch as they are immortal, either suffer or wish themselves to be called gods." *Lactanus 7:17*

Demons

Demons are either fallen angels or very closely associated with them. The Scriptures tell us that demons are powerful (Luke 8:29), evil (Luke 7:21; 8:2), and unclean (Matt. 10:1). They are all under the control of Satan (Matt. 12:24-30). They seek to possess humans (Matt. 8:28-29) and to be worshiped with sacrifices (1 Cor. 10:20). They instigate error/heresy (1 Tim. 4:1) because they don't want men to repent and become Christians (Luke 15:10). They know they will be judged by the saints (1Cor. 6:3) and they know their ultimate destiny (Matt. 8:28-29).

Scripture also teaches that demon possession is not insanity (Matt. 4:24) and it is not a disease (Mark 1:32).

The Bible warns us not to accept the teaching of any angel that contradicts the teaching of Scripture (Galatians 1:8). Fallen angels can appear as holy angels and seem very convincing.

Lucifer's Rebellion

Lucifer's Description

What we know of Lucifer comes mainly from the Biblical books of Isaiah and Ezekiel. According to Ezekiel 28:14, Lucifer was an angel of the cherub class.

We learned in the first chapter that cherubs have the general form of a human, but their heads look more like an ox or bull with horns. They have cloven hooves instead of human feet, and they have four wings (two pairs).

This description has led to the modern idea that the devil has horns and cloven hoofs and is completely red with a pointed tail.

Lucifer's Ancient History

Lucifer was the anointed cherub who covered the throne of God. He was created perfect, sinless like all the other angels. He was the highest of the angels, God's crowning achievement, but then iniquity was found in him.

> "...Thou sealest up the sum, full of wisdom, and perfect in beauty. Thou hast been in Eden the garden of God; every precious stone *was* thy covering, the sardius, topaz, and the diamond, the beryl, the onyx, and the jasper, the sapphire, the emerald, and the carbuncle, and gold: the

workmanship of thy tabrets and of thy pipes was prepared in thee in the day that thou wast created. Thou *art* the anointed cherub that covereth; and I have set thee *so*: thou wast upon the holy mountain of God; thou hast walked up and down in the midst of the stones of fire. Thou *wast* perfect in thy ways from the day that thou wast created, till iniquity was found in thee."
Ezekiel 28:12-15

The prophet Ezekiel tells us Lucifer was in the Garden of Eden. We know he was there when he tempted Eve. Ezekiel also wrote that Lucifer was completely covered with precious stones and he was a great musician. He lived and walked on fiery stones.

When the seventy disciples came back to Jesus, they told Him of their success and that even the demons were subject to them. Not only is Jesus all-powerful, but He is also all knowing. Jesus told them not to rejoice in the power He gave them, but in the fact that they knew the truth. Jesus then told them that He actually witnessed the corruption and fall of Lucifer.

"And he said unto them, I beheld Satan as lightning fall from heaven." *Luke 10:18*

Lucifer's Fall
What happened? How could a being created perfect suddenly, on his own, become corrupted and utterly sinful? In spite of all the riches and power he had, he

wanted more. Ezekiel tells us he was corrupted by his own pride.

> "By the multitude of thy merchandise they have filled the midst of thee with violence, and thou hast sinned: therefore I will cast thee as profane out of the mountain of God: and I will destroy thee, O covering cherub, from the midst of the stones of fire. Thine heart was lifted up because of thy beauty, thou hast corrupted thy wisdom by reason of thy brightness: I will cast thee to the ground, I will lay thee before kings, that they may behold thee." *Ezekiel 28:16-17*

Through his greed and pride he decided he wanted God's position. This thought must have driven him insane. He wanted to rule as God and be worshiped as God. Isaiah records the five "I will's" of Lucifer and the judgment God placed upon him.

> "How art thou fallen from heaven, O Lucifer, son of the morning! *how* art thou cut down to the ground, which didst weaken the [preflood] nations! For thou hast said in thine heart, I will ascend into heaven, I will exalt my throne above the stars of God: I will sit also upon the mount of the congregation, in the sides of the north: I will ascend above the heights of the clouds; I will be like the most High. Yet thou shalt be brought down to hell, to the sides of the pit."
> *Isaiah 14:12-15*

Fallen Angels

Notice that Isaiah seems to indicate Lucifer will be brought down to the sides of the pit of hell because he tried to ascend to godhood. Undoubtedly, those who become convinced they are evolving into gods will suffer the same fate.

Many ancient church fathers teach the Isaiah 14 passage is referring to the fallen cherub, Lucifer. See *Origen OFP 1.5.5* for a detailed discussion of this.

Since Lucifer's fall, Scripture calls him Satan, which is Hebrew for "adversary." In Revelation, John wrote that one third of the angels rebelled along with Lucifer and all were cast out of heaven. This was the first rebellion.

> "And his tail drew the third part of the stars of heaven... And the great dragon was cast out, that old serpent, called the Devil, and Satan, which deceiveth the whole world: he was cast out into the earth, and his angels were cast out with him."
> *Revelation 12:4, 9*

Keep in mind that Lucifer was perfect and the wisest of the angels and still went insane. He literally wanted to replace God in heaven and sit on God's throne.

Lucifer's End
After the Second Coming of Jesus Christ, there will be a thousand year reign on earth and then a new heaven and a new earth. At the end of the millennium, all evil angels,

demons, and men will be cast into the lake of fire permanently.

"[10]And the devil that deceived them was cast into the lake of fire and brimstone, where the beast and the false prophet *are*, and shall be tormented day and night forever and ever." *Revelation 20:10*

Fallen Angels

Azazel's Rebellion

According to the books of *Enoch* and *Jubilees*, in the days of Enoch's father, Jared, the angel Azazel descended to earth. He wanted marriage, children, and possibly to create an empire of his own. After some years of success, a band of two hundred angels, led by an angel named Semyaza, descended on Mount Hermon intent on doing the same thing. Their story is in the next chapter.

God considered angelic marriage, procreation, and empire building a crime against His creation and had Azazel chained under the valley called Beit HaDudo until Judgment Day.

Azazel, the Scapegoat

The interesting thing about Azazel is that he is not only mentioned in the Dead Sea Scrolls, but in the Bible itself. His name appears in the ritual of the scapegoat performed on the Jewish festival of Yom Kippur. During the festival of Yom Kippur, there is a prophetic ceremony that involves two goats. Two nearly-identical goats are selected and brought before the high priest. The high priest places his hands on one of the goats. Another priest brings out the *Qalephi*, a box containing two lots. One of the lots is randomly drawn by the high priest and placed with the first goat. Then the other is withdrawn for the second goat. On one lot is engraved לאדני, meaning "for

Fallen Angels

the Lord." The goat that randomly acquired the lot "for the Lord" is sacrificed for the sins of the people. This animal is a perfect representation of the Messiah dying for the sins of the world. The other lot is engraved with לעזאזל, meaning "for Azazel." This has commonly been translated "scapegoat;" but we have seen that Azazel is actually a proper name, the name of a particular fallen angel. Moses wrote about this ceremony in Leviticus 16 saying:

> And Aaron shall cast lots upon the two goats; one lot for the LORD, and the other lot for the scapegoat. And Aaron shall bring the goat upon which the LORD'S lot fell, and offer him *for* a sin offering. But the goat, on which the lot fell to be the scapegoat, shall be presented alive before the LORD, to make an atonement with him, *and* to let him go for a scapegoat [to Azazel] into the wilderness. *Leviticus 16:8-10*

The Mishnah is a book written about AD 200. It contains the oral Torah, or the exact details explaining how to perform the rituals described in the Old Testament. In *Yoma 4.2* of the Mishnah, details are given concerning the ceremony of the two goats. A scarlet-colored wool cord was especially created for this ceremony. One piece of this cord was tied to one of the horns of the Azazel goat. One piece of the cord was tied around the neck of the Lord's goat.

24

Leviticus describes the Azazel goat being sent into the "wilderness." But the Mishnah gives greater detail about that part of the ritual in *Yoma 6*. The two goats must be alike in appearance, size, and weight. The "wilderness" that the Azazel goat was taken to was actually a ravine twelve miles east of Jerusalem. Between Jerusalem and this ravine were ten stations or booths. Since it was a High Holy Day, one could not travel very far. One priest took the Azazel goat from Jerusalem to the first booth. Then another priest took it from the second to the third booth. This continued until a priest took it from the tenth booth to the ravine. Anciently this ravine was called Beit HaDudo. This is the same place where the *Book of Enoch* states that the fallen angel, Azazel, is bound. It still exists in the Judean desert and is presently called Jabel Muntar. The Mishnah then says the priest took the crimson cord off the goat and tied one piece to the large rock on the cliff of the ravine, and the other piece back onto the horns of the goat. He then pushed the goat off the cliff. Before it would be halfway down the cliff, it was already torn into pieces.

If the ritual was properly done, the crimson cord would turn snow white. At that point, the priest would signal the tenth booth, which would in turn signal the ninth, all the way back to the first booth, which would signal the high priest standing at the door of the sanctuary. When the high priest learned the crimson thread had turned white, he finished the ritual by quoting the prophet Isaiah.

>"'Come now, and let us reason together,' saith the LORD: 'though your sins be as scarlet, they shall be as white as snow; though they be red like crimson, they shall be as wool.'" *Isaiah 1:18*

Then a massive celebration began.

The Meaning of the Ritual

It has been speculated that the scapegoat represents Jesus taking away our sin. That is one possible interpretation. If the information given in the Mishnah is correct, another picture emerges. Two identical goats, one dedicated to God, the other dedicated to Satan. One goat represents the Messiah and the other represents the Antichrist. The only way to tell the difference between the Messiah and the Antichrist is to know the Lord's will by carefully studying the Word of God. At the Second Coming, the Antichrist will be destroyed in Megiddo, in a battle called Armageddon.

Miracles Stopped

In the Babylonian Talmud, *Yoma 40a* states that three miracles occurred connected with the festivals. First, the scarlet cord of the Azazel goat would turn white at his death; second, the gates of the Temple would close by themselves at the end of the Neilah portion of the Day of Atonement ritual; and third, the angel troubled the water (see the chapter on the Great Salvation). The Talmud states these miracles suddenly stopped occurring for some unknown reason about forty years prior to the destruction of the second temple in AD 70. Forty years prior to the destruction of the second temple would be the time the Messiah died, fulfilling the prophecies!

Other Ancient Sources
Barnabas 7 describes the same Azazel ritual but uses the name Rachia for the cliff called Beit HaDudo. Enoch chapters 10, 54, and 55 seem to indicate that Azazel represents the Antichrist in the last days. Azazel (the Antichrist) and all "those who follow him" are ritually bound under Beit HaDudo when the Azazel goat is thrown over the cliff. This could be either that the Antichrist rebels against God in a similar way that Azazel did or one of the children of Azazel, a demon, is the one who possesses the Antichrist.

Conclusion
Even though the ritual of Azazel does teach a prophecy about the coming Antichrist, it is also based on the history of this fallen angel.

Fallen Angels

Semyaza's Rebellion

The *Ancient Book of Enoch* preserved by the Ethiopians and found among the Dead Sea Scrolls contains not only accurate prophecy but also the story of Semyaza. Semyaza and a band of two hundred angels saw what Azazel was doing and decided to do the same. They descended on Ardis, the summit of Mount Hermon, and bound themselves by an oath to take wives, have children, and reshape the world into one of their own making. This was in the days of Jared, Enoch's father, about 460-622 years after Creation.

Azazel had already taken a wife by this time. Some Rabbis taught that his wife was Naamah, daughter of Lamech. (She should not be confused with Naamah, the daughter of Enoch, who was the wife of Noah.) Their descendants were known as the Sedim. The Sedim were a class of pre-flood Nephilim who were worshiped as guardian spirits by the Akkadians. There were even rabbis, according to the Talmud, who invoked these Sedim in rituals for the purpose of exorcism. Azazel began teaching his clan how to make weapons of war, knives, swords, and shields from metal. He also taught jewelry making from earth metals and precious stones, in addition to teaching women to use make-up.

Semyasa and the others taught many other forbidden and twisted things to their wives. They taught sorcery, enchantments, the cutting of roots for poisons and their antidotes, astrology and astronomy, and an intricate religion that set up themselves and their sons to be worshiped in the place of God. One legend states that it was Semyaza who married Naamah, the daughter of Lamech. With such perversion in the land, maybe she was the wife of both Azazel and Semyasa! According to Enoch, the main center of the Nephilim seems to have been at Ardis, the summit of Mount Hermon.

But the story doesn't stop there...

DNA Manipulation

The angels did not stop with simply having children and trying to create empires. They began experimenting with crossbreeding of plants and animals. The *Book of Jasher* states that for those who did not want to become pregnant, there was a well-known drug that caused spontaneous abortions, and, in time, sterility. See the *Ancient Book of Jasher 2:19-22*. There was apparently also a drug used to stop spontaneous abortions. Among the Dead Sea Scrolls there is a little-known fragment of Enoch called the *Book of Giants* (which is added as an appendix in the *Ancient Book of Enoch,* by this author). This work describes exactly how the angels began to crossbreed insects, animals, and humans. They began by taking two hundred sets of creatures with slightly different chromosome counts, like sheep and goats, and crossbred them. Later, they would crossbreed sets of the new unstable life forms to create further modifications, then repeat to get the desired effect. In Genesis 1 God said "after its own kind" ten times. This mixing of kinds was complete rebellion against God's laws of reproduction.

The Result

To crush this second rebellion, God held Azazel responsible for all this wickedness and chained him under the valley Beit HaDudo. God then commanded the holy angels to cause a civil war between the Nephilim clans. After the Nephilim were completely annihilated, Semyasa, and those who fell with him, were chained in Tartarus, a special place in hell. The disembodied spirits of the Nephilim were allowed to roam the earth and became known as demons.

Revelation 9:14 informs us that there are four mighty angels that are chained under the Euphrates River. We do not know the story of these angels, but most likely they were part of this second rebellion. It may also mean that when they are released, they will again create hybrid creatures.

Modern DNA Manipulation

Today we are following in the same misguided footsteps as our ancestors. We are beginning to tamper with God's creation. Here are just a few examples:

In 1978, the first report of the birth of a baby from in vitro fertilization came from England. That same year in the US, the National Institutes of Health approved field experiments using altered bacteria.

Fallen Angels

In 1980, the U. S. Supreme Court ruled that the U. S. Patent and Trademark Office could legally grant a patent on a genetically engineered "oil-eating" bacteria. Since then, hundreds of patents have been issued on genetically modified bacteria, viruses, and plants.

In 1988, a patent was granted on mice that contained a cancer-predisposing gene. These mice would always develop cancer upon reaching maturity. They are currently used to test cancer-treating drugs.

In 1997, the first sheep and monkey were cloned. President Bill Clinton then signed a law making it illegal to experiment with, or clone, a human being.

In 2002, scientists successfully added a gene from a jellyfish to a mouse, creating the first glow-in-the-dark mouse. Later, this was also done successfully on cats, guinea pigs, and monkeys.

In 2008, a mouse that had been frozen for sixteen years was cloned. The clone has reproduced four normal mice. Based on this procedure, scientists are trying to clone a perfectly preserved woolly mammoth found frozen in Siberia, and thereby bring back this extinct animal.

The Pyrenean Ibex became extinct in 2000. It was cloned in 2009, but the clone died nine minutes after birth due to lung damage.

In England, the 2008 Human Fertilization Embryology Act was passed allowing researchers to create human-animal hybrid embryos, as long as they were destroyed after fourteen days. This Act was to research how stem cells could possibly cure certain diseases. Over one hundred and fifty hybrid embryos have been created, both cybrids (human nucleus implanted into an animal cell) and chimeras (animal nucleus implanted into a human cell).

By the year 2012, a process was developed to genetically alter a cow's DNA to produce human antibodies instead of cow antibodies. This was done by taking two strands of human DNA and putting them into a mouse to replicate. At a certain stage of development, these cells were removed and implanted into a chicken, which allowed them to be combined in a specific way. They were then removed from the chicken and placed into a hamster. The hamster cell line allowed for one last modification, and then it was transferred into the cow after the cow's immune system had been neutralized. The original cow was then cloned. As a result, scientists were able to produce an unlimited supply of human antibodies in case of an epidemic outbreak.

We have begun a spiral to disaster. We are able to bring back extinct species; we have created new bacteria and plants. We have begun to create new animal species. We now have glowing mice, cats, and monkeys and partly-human cows that produce human antibodies. The Lord must return soon, for the Scripture says:

"[37]But as the days of Noe were, so shall also the coming of the Son of man be." *Matthew 24:37*

Nephilim History

The history of the Nephilim starts with the sons of God in Genesis 6; but we can pull information from the Bible, Josephus, Jasher, Enoch, Jubilees, and some Dead Sea Scrolls and paint a fairly complete picture of the history of the giants.

> "And it came to pass, when men began to multiply on the face of the earth, and daughters were born unto them, that the sons of God saw the daughters of men that they *were* fair; and they took them wives of all which they chose. And the LORD said, My Spirit will not always strive with man, for that he also *is* flesh: yet his days will be an hundred and twenty years. There were giants [Nephilim] in the earth in those days; and also after that, when the sons of God came in unto the daughters of men, and they bare *children* to them, the same *became* mighty men which *were* of old, men of renown."
> *Genesis 6:1-4*

The *Book of Enoch* gives a detailed account of the two hundred angels who fell and corrupted all flesh by genetically tampering with animals and mankind. We have seen that these angels married human women. Their children, half angelic and half human, became known as Nephilim. This was an abomination before God. Jude 6-7 states that the angels were bound for committing the same sin that the men of Sodom wanted to do with the angels

Fallen Angels

(Genesis 19:1-5). He then quotes the prophecy in Enoch 1:9. Second Peter 2:4 states these angels are bound in a place called Tartarus (hell in the KJV). According to Enoch 22, this is the special place for holding *only* these angels, their wives, and their sons until the judgment.

For the complete story of the two hundred, see Enoch 6-16. They descended in the days of Jared (460-622 AM; 3465-3303 BC).

> "And their judges and rulers went to the daughters of men and took their wives by force from their husbands according to their choice, and the sons of men, in those days, took from the cattle of the earth the beasts of the field, and the fowls of the air, and taught the mixture of the animals of one species with another..." *Jasher 4.18*

> "For owing to these three things came the flood upon the earth, namely, owing to the fornication wherein the Watchers against the law of their ordinances went a whoring after the daughters of men, and took themselves wives of all which they chose: and they made the beginning of uncleanness. And they begot sons, the Naphilim, and they were all unlike, and they devoured one another: and the giants slew the Naphil, and the Naphil slew the Eljo, and the Eljo, mankind, and one man another... And after this they sinned against the beasts and birds..." *Jubilees 7.18-25*

"For many angels of God accompanied with women, and begot sons that proved unjust, and despisers of all that was good, on account of the confidence they had in their own strength; for the tradition is, that these men did what resembled the acts of those whom the Grecians call giants or Titans." *Josephus Ant. 1.3.1*

"In Hebron there were till then left the race of giants, who had bodies so large, and countenances so entirely different from other men, that they were surprising to the sight, and terrible to the hearing. The bones of these men are still shown to this very day." *Josephus Ant. 5.2.3*

Notice that Josephus records that the Greek legends of the Titans were based on Nephilim history. *Jubilees 10:1-12* informs us that after the Flood evil spirits began afflicting many of Noah's descendants. Noah prayed to God to bind all of the demons away from men. God bound nine-tenths of the demons, leaving only one-tenth to tempt and torment man. Revelation 9 tells us that the demons will be released during the Great Tribulation. This will be the other nine-tenths of them. If the angels are bound, and the Nephilim are disembodied spirits, where did the giants after the flood come from? A third rebellion? No. The story continues:

Genesis tells us that after the flood Noah divided the planet among his three sons. Ham was given what we call Africa and Shem, the middle east. Canaan, Ham's son, left his territory and ventured north along the Mediterranean Sea. Why did Canaan travel all the way up the coast to found Sidon, his first city, in an area he knew was not his territory, then quickly settle another city, Tyre?

The map at the right shows that those two locations are the closest he could get to mount an expedition to Mount Hermon. He wanted to find information about the pre-flood giants!

> "And Canaan grew, and his father taught him writing, and he went to seek for himself a place where he might seize for himself a city. And he found a writing which former (generations) had carved on the rock, and he read what was thereon, and he transcribed it and sinned owing to it; for it contained the teaching of the Watchers in accordance with which they used to observe the omens of the sun and moon and stars in all the signs of heaven. And he wrote it down and said nothing regarding it; for he was afraid to speak to Noah about it lest he should be angry with him on account of it." *Jubilees 8.1-5*

After finding the writing containing the science of the Watchers, Canaan sought to create a race of warrior giants using the same type of genetic tampering which was done before the Flood. This explains how the giants came to be, but with a few problems. Second Samuel 21:20 describes giants with six fingers on each hand and six toes on each foot. Moses led the children of Israel into battle with Og, the king of Bashan, who being a true giant, stood at least twelve feet tall (Deuteronomy 3:11). Bashan was anciently called the Land of the Giants. Og actually reigned from Mt. Hermon (Joshua 12:4-5), the place where the angels descended. Even up to King David's time, Goliath remained (1 Samuel 17:4). He was one-quarter giant and three-quarters Philistine and reached only nine feet, nine inches tall. Another race of giants were the Anakim (Numbers 13:21-33). Some of the Amorites were as tall as a cedar tree (Amos 2:9), probably referring to the sons of Anak. Other giant races found in the Old Testament included the Emim (Deuteronomy 2:9-11), and the Zamzummim (Deuteronomy 2:20-21). The Anakim, Emim, and the Zamzummim were all equally tall. The Valley of Hinnom was anciently called the Valley of Giants (Joshua 15:8; 18:16).

Joshua destroyed all the Anakim except for a giant who escaped to Gaza (Joshua 11:21-22), the later home of Goliath. David's men killed Goliath's brother and one other son of the giant (2 Samuel 21:20-21). In four hundred years time the giant out bred, so that Goliath and his brothers were only nine feet tall instead of thirteen feet tall.

The Genesis 6 word for giants (Nephilim) occurs in only one other place: Numbers 13:33. These same post-flood

Fallen Angels

giants who are called *Nephilim* in Numbers, are referred to as *Rephaim* in Deuteronomy 2:11 and Genesis 14:5. These passages show that the post-flood giants were a special kind of Nephilim called Rephaim. This means they were not the procreation of another angelic rebellion, but a genetic tampering by man in a similar fashion as the angels did in the pre-flood world.

Demonic Possession
Demons seek to possess human beings. There are numerous Scripture passages that discuss demonic possession and exorcism (casting out a demon).

Demonic spirits possess men (Matthew 12:43); they know God, Jesus, and the prophecies (Mark 1:23); they can give supernatural strength and cause people to cut themselves (Mark 5:2-5); they are under the control of Satan (Mark 7:25-26; Luke 4:33); and sometimes cause disease (Luke 9:42).

> "[19]Behold, I give unto you power to tread on serpents and scorpions, and over all the power of the enemy: and nothing shall by any means hurt you." *Luke 10:19*

The Ancient Church Fathers on Demonic Possession
We can surmise from the following quotes that the ancient church taught Christians cannot be possessed. Even new Christians can easily cast out demons. Christians are not to be involved in occult matters, but instead, free people by sharing the gospel with them.

Tertullian 190-210 AD

Apology 23 - Moreover, if sorcerers put dreams into people's minds by the power of the angels and demons whose aid they have invited, how much more likely is this power of evil. ... The wicked spirit, bidden to speak by a follower of Christ, will as readily make the truthful confession that he is a demon.

Apology 35 - The arts of astrologers, soothsayers, augurs, and magicians were made known by the angels who sinned, and are forbidden by God.

Marcion 1.18 - The Marcionites are very strongly addicted to astrology.

Treatise of the Soul 1.57 - Magic and sorcery only seem to raise the dead. Only God can really raise the dead.

Lactantius 285 AD

Divine Institutes 2.15 - There are angels and different kinds of demons. Demons are also called Jinn by some.

Divine Institutes 2.16 - Demons have no power over Christians, and will tell the truth if so commanded by a Christian.

Divine Institutes 2.17 - Astrology, soothsaying, divination, oracles, necromancy, and the art of magic are the invention of demons and vain. Magicians and enchanters call demons by their true names and mingle false things with the truth.

Divine Institutes 4.27 - Even the Greek gods flee when the name of Jesus is used. If a god is commanded to tell the truth, it confesses that it is a demon. If one could call up Jupiter or one of the others from the dead, they would confess they were men, and not gods, and that there is only one true God. The spirits that pretend to be them, lie.

Origen 230 AD

Against Celsus 3.28 - The Greek god Apollo is a demon.

Against Celsus 3:36 - All angels, demons, and other unseen powers are subject to the name of Jesus.

Against Celsus 4:93 - There are different species of demons.

Against Celsus 7:3 - A true prophet under the control of the Holy Spirit does not fall into ecstasy, or madness, like the pagans do.

Against Celsus 7:4 - Every Christian, even a new one, has no problem casting out demons.

Spiritual Warfare

Spiritual warfare is fighting or standing against Satan. We have seen that demonic possession is nothing for a Christians to worry about. So how does Satan attack? He doesn't attack by sending an army of possessed people with guns to kill us all. He attacks by spreading lies and deception.

Satan's Attack

The Scriptures teach that Satan and his kingdom have little power over Christians. Therefore, the only way he has to attack believers is by spreading false doctrine in order to divide and confuse us. He causes those under his control to persecute Christians. He wants to stop the spread of the gospel so that no one can be saved.

"[31]And the Lord said, Simon, Simon, behold, Satan hath desired *to have* you, that he may sift *you* as wheat: [32]But I have prayed for thee, that thy faith fail not: and when thou art converted, strengthen thy brethren." *Luke 22:31-32*

"And lest I should be exalted above measure through the abundance of the revelations, there was given to me a thorn in the flesh, the messenger of Satan to buffet me, lest I should be exalted above measure." *2 Corinthians 12:7*

"[10]Fear none of those things which thou shalt suffer: behold, the devil shall cast *some* of you into prison, that ye may be tried; and ye shall have tribulation ten days: be thou faithful unto death, and I will give thee a crown of life.
Revelation 2:10

"[18]Wherefore we would have come unto you, even I Paul, once and again; but Satan hindered us." *1 Thessalonians 2:18*

He also tempts us to sin, which brings disease and other consequences.

"[16]And ought not this woman, being a daughter of Abraham, whom Satan hath bound, lo, these eighteen years, be loosed from this bond on the Sabbath day?" *Luke 13:16*

Ignorance of God's Word
People are deceived into persecuting Christians (even if they think they are true Christians themselves) by being ignorant of God's Word.

"[12]...then cometh the devil, and taketh away the word out of their hearts, lest they should believe and be saved." *Luke 8:12*

People are told what the Word is *supposed* to say, but they never read it for themselves. Or they read a little of it, then put it down and follow someone on TV, trusting some other voice to bring them close to God. But that never works.

"[13]For such *are* false apostles, deceitful workers, transforming themselves into the apostles of Christ. [14]And no marvel; for Satan himself is transformed into an angel of light. [15]Therefore *it is* no great thing if his ministers also be transformed as the ministers of righteousness; whose end shall be according to their works."
2 Corinthians 11:13-15

"[10]But these speak evil of those things which they know not: but what they know naturally, as brute beasts, in those things they corrupt themselves."
Jude 1:10

"[3]But I fear, lest by any means, as the serpent beguiled Eve through his subtilty, so your minds should be corrupted from the simplicity that is in Christ." *2 Corinthians 11:3*

"But though we, or an angel from heaven, preach any other gospel unto you than that which we have preached unto you, let him be accursed."
Galatians 1:8

Satan even tries to put these deceivers into the pulpit or at least put someone in the pulpit who doesn't understand Satan's tactics. Many people twist Scripture for their own ends.

"[8]Be sober, be vigilant; because your adversary the devil, as a roaring lion, walketh about, seeking whom he may devour:" *1 Peter 5:8*

"[6]Not a novice, lest being lifted up with pride he fall into the condemnation of the devil. [7]Moreover he must have a good report of them which are without; lest he fall into reproach and the snare of the devil." *1 Timothy 3:6-7*

Satan twisted what God had said in order to tempt Eve and make her doubt God.

"hath God said, Ye shall not eat of every tree of the garden?" *Genesis 3:1*

Satan misquoted the Scripture to Jesus to get Him to fall. Satan even tried to use psychology to influence Jesus to sin in order that he might help people.

"[6]And saith unto him, If thou be the Son of God, cast thyself down: for it is written, He shall give his angels charge concerning thee: and in *their* hands they shall bear thee up, lest at any time thou dash thy foot against a stone." *Matthew 4:6*

In Numbers 22, Balaam was greedy for gold. The pagan king Balak offered him gold if he would curse Israel; but God continued to bless Israel. So Balaam devised a plan to lead Israel into sin so God would be angry and curse

them. This is a classic trap of Satan: get us to sin in some
way just to miss out on God's blessings.

The Christian's Defense
We need to recognize that we are not fighting other
people. We are fighting the invisible demonic powers that
are controlling those people. Those people Satan uses to
attack us need our help to escape an eternity in hell.

> "For we wrestle not against flesh and blood, but
> against principalities, against powers, against the
> rulers of the darkness of this world, against
> spiritual wickedness in high *places*."
> *Ephesians 6:12*

> "⁷Submit yourselves therefore to God. Resist the
> devil, and he will flee from you." *James 4:7*

> "¹⁹Behold, I give unto you power to tread on
> serpents and scorpions, and over all the power of
> the enemy: and nothing shall by any means hurt
> you." *Luke 10:19*

What are Our Weapons?
First, we must forgive those people who hurt us and try to
help them. We do not want to fall into Satan's trap of
fighting the wrong fight.

> "¹⁰To whom ye forgive anything, I *forgive* also:
> for if I forgave anything, to whom I forgave *it*, for
> your sakes *forgave I it* in the person of Christ;

Fallen Angels

> [11]Lest Satan should get an advantage of us: for we are not ignorant of his devices."
> *2 Corinthians 2:10-11*

> "[11]And they overcame him by the blood of the Lamb, and by the word of their testimony; and they loved not their lives unto the death."
> *Revelation 12:11*

We fight spiritual warfare by teaching proper doctrine. That is what frees people. Everyone desiring salvation must become a Christian and *obey* the teachings of Jesus Christ.

> "[4](For the weapons of our warfare *are* not carnal, but mighty through God to the pulling down of strong holds;) [5]casting down imaginations, and every high thing that exalteth itself against the knowledge of God, and bringing into captivity every thought to the obedience of Christ; [6]and having in a readiness to revenge all disobedience, when your obedience is fulfilled."
> *2 Corinthians 10:4-6*

We must understand two things: salvation is only through Jesus Christ and no other religion tells the truth. We must practice righteousness and spread the gospel to everyone. We must continue in our faith as taught by the Word of God, and use the Word of God to destroy the lies of all the false religions and cults that are damning people to an eternal hell.

"[11]Put on the whole armour of God, that ye may be able to stand against the wiles of the devil. ... [14]Stand therefore, having your loins girt about with truth, and having on the breastplate of righteousness; [15]and your feet shod with the preparation of the gospel of peace; [16]above all, taking the shield of faith, wherewith ye shall be able to quench all the fiery darts of the wicked. [17]And take the helmet of salvation, and the sword of the Spirit, which is the word of God:"
Ephesians 6:11,14-17

We must have the Word in our hearts and minds to be effective in Spiritual warfare.

"[14]I have written unto you, fathers, because ye have known Him *that is* from the beginning. I have written unto you, young men, because ye are strong, and the word of God abideth in you, and ye have overcome the wicked one." *1 John 2:14*

Greatest Lies from Satan

Ecumenicism
"All religions are the same, they all lead to salvation."

"[20]But *I say*, that the things which the Gentiles sacrifice, they sacrifice to devils, and not to God: and I would not that ye should have fellowship with devils. [21]Ye cannot drink the cup of the Lord,

and the cup of devils: ye cannot be partakers of the Lord's table, and of the table of devils."
1 Corinthians 10:20-21

"¹⁴Be ye not unequally yoked together with unbelievers: for what fellowship hath righteousness with unrighteousness? and what communion hath light with darkness? ¹⁵And what concord hath Christ with Belial? or what part hath he that believeth with an infidel?"
2 Corinthians 6:14-15

You Don't Have To Believe in the Trinity
Jesus stated He is the "I AM." This is the name God used when He spoke to Moses from the burning bush in Exodus 3:14. All Christian denomination believe in the Trinity. It is clearly taught in Scripture. All Christian cults deny the doctrine of the trinity. They have just enough poison to send their followers to hell.

"²⁴I said therefore unto you, that ye shall die in your sins: for if ye believe not that I am *he*, ye shall die in your sins." *John 8:24*

You Don't Have to Stop Sinning
We cannot willfully continue to practice sin if the Holy Spirit is in our lives. This includes the sin of not continuing to study the Word of God to keep ourselves pure.

"⁹Whosoever is born of God doth not commit sin; for His seed remaineth in him: and he cannot sin, because he is born of God." *1 John 3:9*

You Don't Have to Study God's Word

Since we all have a sin nature that corrupts our thought patterns, we can only know what is truly right from studying the Scriptures. If we know we can be influenced by the demonic realm, then we must renew our mind daily by the Word of God.

"¹⁵Study to shew thyself approved unto God, a workman that needeth not to be ashamed, rightly dividing the word of truth." *2 Timothy 2:15*

"³¹Then said Jesus to those Jews which believed on Him, If ye continue in My word, *then* are ye My disciples indeed;" *John 8:31*

"²⁶That He might sanctify and cleanse it with the washing of water by the word," *Ephesians 5:26*

"⁵Not by works of righteousness which we have done, but according to His mercy He saved us, by the washing of regeneration, and renewing of the Holy Ghost;" *Titus 3:5*

Other Demonic Doctrines

Satan will have his own religious doctrines (Revelation 3:8-9) that blind peoples' minds from the truth (2 Corinthians 4:4). These are usually connected with idols (1 Corinthians 8).

Fallen Angels

Vegetarianism and celibacy are two demonic doctrines that will manifest in the last days.

> [1]Now the Spirit speaketh expressly, that in the latter times some shall depart from the faith, giving heed to seducing spirits, and doctrines of devils; [2]Speaking lies in hypocrisy; having their conscience seared with a hot iron; [3]Forbidding to marry, *and commanding* to abstain from meats, which God hath created to be received with thanksgiving of them which believe and know the truth. *1 Timothy 4:1-3*

Paul stated that a good minister will always teach that Jesus was God manifested in the flesh, sinless, resurrected, and ascended. These are cardinal doctrines that must be believed and taught for salvation. This means these doctrines will be demonically attacked with great ferocity.

> [16]And without controversy great is the mystery of godliness: God was manifest in the flesh, justified in the Spirit, seen of angels, preached unto the Gentiles, believed on in the world, received up into glory. *1 Timothy 3:16*

Dictionary of Angels and Demons

Fallen Angels

Abaddon: (the destroyer)
See *Angel of the Bottomless Pit.*

Abracadabra: (I bless the dead)
This ancient magic word is used in amulets to ward off sickness. It means "I bless the dead." It is said to be derived from the Hebrew phrase "HaBrachah dabarah" meaning "speak the blessing." This word was used by the Gnostic Basilides to invoke his god, Abraxas.

Abraxas:
Ancient Egyptian Christians listed Abraxas as a demon. The Basilidian Gnostics worshiped him as their supreme god and used the word Abracadabra in his invocation.

Adam:
Adam was the first man God created. Since he was directly created by God, he is sometimes referred to as a son of God.

Adimus:
Adimus was one of the angels the Roman Catholic Church excommunicated in the Council of Lateran in AD 745. Other reprobate angels included Uriel, Raguel, Simiel, and others. Bishops who approved their veneration were excommunicated. See *Reprobated Angels*.

Fallen Angels

Aeon:

In Gnosticism an aeon was one of the highest emanations of God. Abraxis was said to be head over the aeons.

Ahiah: (Hahya, Yahweh is life)
Ahiah was the son of the fallen angel Semyaza, according to the *Ancient Book of Enoch* and *Legends of the Jews*.

Allah:

Allah was a moon god worshiped in ancient pagan Arabia. The moon god had three daughters al-Lat, al-Uzza and Manat. Allah is also the name of the supreme god of the Muslims.

AL Lat, Al Ussa:

Al Lat and Al Ussa were crane angels / goddesses in ancient pagan Arabia. They were two of the daughters of the moon god who were prayed to for intercession. Mohammad ordered their idols destroyed. In the Quran, surah 53, their names are mentioned. They are two of the daughters of Allah. The other one was Manat.

Amber:

The Hebrew word translated amber in the Ezekiel 1:4 KJV is considered by some rabbis to be a fire-speaking class of angel similar to Seraphim.

Amulet:

A piece of jewelry that is supposed to ward off evil by its magic power.

Anakim: (giants)
1) Before the Flood, the name that fallen angels Uzza and Azael gave to their offspring, according to the *Zohar*. The Hebrews called them Nephilim (Genesis 6).
2) After the Flood, a race of giants who settled in the hill country of Judah.

Ancient of Days:
A title for God the Father, given in Daniel 7:9, described as having a white robe, hair like white wool, and eyes like flaming fire.

Angel:
The Hebrew word "malak" means messenger. These are spirit messengers between God and man. Two angels named in the Old and New Testaments are Gabriel and Michael. The cherub Lucifer is also mentioned. In the Old Testament Apocrypha the angels Uriel and Raphael are also recorded. See the chapter on the *Creation of Angels* for full details.

Angels of the Ark of the Covenant:
The mercy seat on the top of the Ark of the Covenant has two cherubs, one on the left hand and one on the right, facing each other. Jewish legend says these are Zarall and Jael.

Angel of the Bottomless Pit:
This is the demon who is lord of the locusts released from the abyss to torment mankind for five months. (Revelation 9:1-13). His name in Greek is Apollyon /

Apollo and in Hebrew it is Abaddon, meaning the destroyer.

Angel of Death:
The angel who passed over Egypt at the time of the Exodus and killed all the firstborn sons. See chapter on the *Creation of Angels*.

Angel of Fire:
Hebrews 1:7 refers to angels as ministering spirits and flames of fire. In Revelation 14:18 we see an angel that has power over fire. Some rabbis teach that just as Adam was made out of earth, angels were made out of fire.

Angel of His Presence:
Isaiah 63:9-10 is a reference to either the pre-incarnate Jesus Christ or the Holy Spirit.

Angel of Light:
An angel that brings knowledge. In 2 Corinthians 11:14 Satan can appear as an angel of light to deceive.

Angels of the Vials of Wrath:
In Revelation 15-16, these seven angels destroy that which remains of the Antichrist's system during the seven-year tribulation period.

Angel Who Troubled the Water:
John 5:4 records that an angel performed a miracle each year (prior to the Living Water ceremony) where he

would trouble the water at the pool of Bethesda healing the first person into the pool of whatever disease he had. The Talmud states this and other miracles stopped occurring about forty years before the temple was destroyed, which is the time of the Messiah's death on the cross.

Anointed Cherub:
The title of Satan given in Ezekiel 28:14. This shows Satan is a fallen angel of the Cherub class.

Antichrist:
The name of the possessed person (1 John 2:18, 22; 4:3; and 2 John 7) who leads the world in the last great rebellion against God during the time known as the Great Tribulation. This occurs immediately prior to the Second Coming of Jesus Christ.

Apparition:
The manifestation of a spirit or ghost where everyone in the room sees it.

Apollo:
The Greek god of the sun, long hair, and the locust. When referring to Apollo as the god of the locust, he is called the "destroyer." See *Angel of the Bottomless Pit*.

Apollyon:
See *Angel of the Bottomless Pit*.

Fallen Angels

Archangel:
A rank of heavenly spirit just above the angel. Daniel
10:13 referred to Michael as a "chief prince" or
archangel. Jude 9 called Michael an archangel. In 1
Thessalonians 4:16 we see an archangel involved in the
rapture of the church. Revelation 8:2 refers to seven
angels who stand before God. The *Ancient Book of
Enoch* names these seven archangels as: Uriel, Raguel,
Michael, Seraqael, Gabriel, Haniel, and Raphael.

Archons: (rulers)
Spirit rulers who are set over nations and worlds in the
Gnostic religion.

Arelim:
A variant spelling of the Erelim.

Arioc: (Ariukh, Oriockh, Arioch)
Jewish legend stated he was the guardian angel of Enoch
and his descendants. He was appointed by God to
preserve Enoch's writings.

Armen:
One of the fallen angels listed in *Enoch* 69.

Asharah:
A goddess worshiped by the Hebrews in times of
apostasy. Her priestesses used drugs to manipulate the
populace (Ezekiel 13:17-21). She may be the same as
the demoness Lillith.

Asmodeus: (creature of judgment)
A demon that tormented Sarah and her fiancés in the apocryphal book of Tobit 3:8. In Jewish legend, he is a demon of impurity and is connected with the Greek god Saturn.

Asshur:
Son of Shem and father of the Assyrians. Later he was deified and worshiped as their chief god.

Astaroth:
Jewish legend states he is a fallen seraph and was worshiped as a god in ancient Syria.

Astarte:
Astarte was also called Astaroth, Ashtoreth, Ishtar, and Venus. She was the chief goddess worshiped by the Phoenicians, Syrians, and Carthaginians. She was the moon goddess of fertility worshiped by the Israelites in times of apostasy (2 Kings 23:13). Jeremiah stated her worshipers referred to her as the "queen of heaven."

Azael:
An alternate spelling of Azazel. He is said to have cohabited with Naamah, Lamech's daughter (Genesis 4:19-22) and their children were known as the Sedim clan of Nephilim. After the Flood the Sedim were venerated by the Assyrians as guardian spirits.

Fallen Angels

Azazel: (God strengthens)

A mighty fallen angel who is referred to as the scapegoat in Leviticus 16:8. He was the leader of the second rebellion and is chained under the valley of Beit HaDudo until Judgment Day. Ancient church father Irenaeus referred to him as that "fallen yet mighty angel." The ancient rabbis stated he was the chief of the bene elim. They were also called the Sedim, lower angels, or "men spirits."

Azza: (strong)

Another name for the fallen angel Semyaza.

ℬ

Baal: (Lord)

Originally a Semitic word meaning lord. Later in the Old Testament, Adonai was used exclusively for Yahweh and Baal was used exclusively for the Canaanite god. Each Canaanite city had its own lord and princess respectively called Baal and (h)asharah. The "h" from the Hebrew word meaning "the princess" dropped off and the word became Asharah. Originally the Canaanite religion was based on the concept of ancestor worship and the concept of evolving into gods. In some cultures Baal was a moon god and had three daughters. See Allah.

Baal-Peor: (lord of the opening, lord of Mt. Peor)

A fertility god worshiped by the Moabites in Numbers 25:1-3. Some church fathers connect him with the Greek Priapus.

Barakel:

One of the two hundred fallen angels of the second rebellion, according to Enoch. His son was Mahwey. One of the main corruptions Barakel taught was astrology.

Bashan:

The Golan heights, anciently called the Land of the Giants. It was ruled over by King Og whose bed measured approximately thirteen and a half feet long.

Fallen Angels

Beelzebub: (lord of the flies)

The god worshiped in Ekron, Philista, and Syria in 2 Kings 1:3. He is called the prince of demons in Matthew 10:25; Mark 3:22; and Luke 11:15; and the prince of devils in Matthew 12:24. Valentinian Gnostics called him the "lord of chaos."

Behemoth:

A creature mentioned in Job 40; this large land animal or dinosaur became the symbol of the end time apostasy, along with the leviathan. See *Leviathan*.

Belial: (Bel is god, Beliar, Berial)

This demon is mentioned by Paul in 2 Corinthians 6:15. "What has Christ to do with Belial?" This is a descriptive way of saying Christians should have nothing to do with anything connected with idolatry.

Beliar:

Another name for Belial.

Bene Elim:

Another spelling of Bene Elohim

Bene Elohim: (sons of God)

Angels and archangels. See Genesis 6:2. In some rabbinic commentaries they are not angels or archangels, but ischim.

Brazen Serpent:

Numbers 21:8, 9 records God commanding Moses to create a brazen serpent. All who looked at it would be healed from snake bite. Later, some Israelites thought a residue of the power to heal might be still in it and began to venerate it. When godly king Hezekiah found out that the brazen serpent had become an idol, he had it destroyed (2 Kings 18:4).

Fallen Angels

C

Calf:

Israel worshiped a golden calf when they came out of Egypt (Exodus 32:7-8) and Jeroboam created calves to worship (1 Kings 12:26-33). Jeroboam reinstituted their worship on the fifteenth of the second month. See Halloween

Captain of the Host of the Lord:

A Christophany that occurred in Joshua 5. This being was obviously not an angel because He received Joshua's worship.

Chemosh:

A Moabite fire god to whom children were sacrificed. Solomon built an altar to him in 1 Kings 11:7. He was worshiped by the Moabites (Num. 21:29; Jer. 48:46) and the Ammonites (Judges 11:12, 24). He is sometimes connected with the god Milcom (Malcolm).

Cherubim:

A class of angel having four wings, cloven hooves, and a face similar to an ox with horns (Ezekiel 10:14). The term Cherubim occurs ninety-one times in the Hebrew Old Testament. Lucifer is a fallen cherub according to Ezekiel 28:14-15. One guarded the entrance to the garden of Eden in Genesis 3:24. King Solomon had two large cherubim created for the holy place (1 Kings 6:23-29).

Christ:

Daniel prophesied the "Christ" or "Messiah" would come before the destruction of the second temple (Daniel 9:26). Jesus Christ is the second person of the Trinity and the Son of God the Father.

Christophany:

A pre-incarnate appearance of Christ. This pre-incarnate appearance is also called an theophany.

Chiun:

A star god the Israelites secretly worshiped in the wilderness, as mentioned in Amos 5:25-27. Called Remphan by Stephan in Acts 7:43, it was probably associated with Saturn.

Comforter, the:

A name for the Holy Spirit, third person of the Trinity, found in John 14:26.

Curse:

Biblically a curse takes place when God is displeased with a group of people and prophesies that if they continue in their sin, they will be punished. Joshua 6:26 tells us that Joshua, through inspiration of the Holy Spirit, cursed the man who would rebuild Jericho. This was a prophecy that was fulfilled in 1 Kings 16:34. There is no such thing as a curse placed upon Christians by any evil being. (Proverbs 26:2)

Daemon:
The Greek word for demon.

Dagon:
The chief god of the Phoenicians and Philistines, and the god of the city Ashdod (1 Samuel 5:1-7). He is pictured as half man and half fish.

Daughters of men:
The wives of the sons of God and the mothers of the Nephilim. See chapter on *Azazel's Rebellon*.

Day Star:
Another name for Lucifer found in some translations of Isaiah 14:12.

Death Angels:
Angels that are sent by God to destroy armies or people. One angel destroyed 185,000 Assyrians in one night. One angel killed the first born of all men and animals in the tenth plague of Egypt. See the chapter on the *Creation of Angels*.

Demon:
Spirits of the Nephilim, now under the control of Satan, who seek to corrupt the minds of men and possess their bodies.

Fallen Angels

Demonic Possession:
Possession by a demon. See *Possession*.

Destroyer, the:
Another name for Abaddon. See *Angel of the Bottomless Pit*.

Devil:
From the Greek Diabolus, a name for Satan. It is similar in meaning to Satan, the Adversary. The devil is symbolized as a dragon and serpent (Revelation 20:2).

Divination:
The practice of invoking a spirit or power or using an occult device to determine future events. Examples are astrology, tarot cards, ouija boards, etc. See also *Wizard* and *Necromancer*.

Dragon:
A name for the devil in Revelation 12:9.

Dobbiel:
Another name for Dubbiel.

Dubbiel: (bear god).

El:
A Hebrew word for God.

Elect One:
A name for the Messiah in the *Book of Enoch.*

Elioud:
One of the three clans of Nephilim.

Evil Spirit:
Another term for a demonic spirit. These spirits are under the control of Satan and are also called unclean spirits.

Exorcism:
The process of making a demon leave a human being he is possessing. This is very easy when a true Christian is present. See chapter on *Spiritual Warfare.*

Eblis: (despair)
A name for Satan in Arabic lore, although they have him as a jinn rather than a fallen angel.

Elim: (mighty ones)
An order of angels in rabbinic literature.

Elyon: (the most high)

Fallen Angels

Elohim:

A term used mainly for Yahweh, but occasionally for angels.

Erelim: (Arelim, valiant ones)

A class of angel sometimes described as white fire. The Hebrew word is translated as valiant ones in Isaiah 33:7 KJV.

Fallen Angels:
Revelation 12:4 reveals that one-third of God's angels fell in Lucifer's rebellion. See chapter on *Lucifer's Rebellion.*

False Prophet, the:
The satanic religious leader in the last days who causes everyone to worship the Antichrist. See Revelation 16:13; 19:20; 20:10.

Familiar Spirit:
The most famous medium who had a "familiar spirit" was the medium of Endor found in 1 Samuel 28:7. She conjured up the spirit of Samuel to speak with King Saul. This act is forbidden in Deuteronomy 18:10, 11. This Canaanite practice, called "Ob" in Hebrew, was to create a necromantic pit and use incantations to make a spirit materialize for all to view. Some of these used a teraphim.

Female Angel:
The Bible seems to indicate there are no female angels. They rarely appear in Jewish, Arabic, and Persian lore.

Female Demon:
If the Nephilim were children of the sons of God (angels) and women, then they would have been male and female children. Since God cursed their spirits to be

earthbound, those demons would have the male and female personalities they had in physical form. One female demon mentioned in Scripture is Lillith found in Isaiah 34:14. Her name is translated as "Screech owl" in the KJV.

G

Gabriel: (God is my strength)

Gabriel is the angel who announced to Zacharias that he would be the father of the forerunner of the Messiah in Luke 1:19, and to Mary that she would be the mother of the Messiah in Luke 1:26. Gabriel also revealed many prophecies to the prophet Daniel in Daniel 8:16 and Daniel 9:21-12:13. Gabriel and Michael were two angels who fought with the Prince of Persia (Daniel 10:13). The court testimony of Joan of Arc indicates that Joan stated it was Gabriel who instructed her to go to the King of France.

Gehenna:

One of two words translated hell in the New Testament. The other is Hades. Hades is the Greek word for the Hebrew word sheol, meaning the abode of the dead. Gehenna refers to the lake of fire that all unsaved humans, fallen angels, and demons will be thrown into after their judgment. See Revelation 20:14.

Genii: (sing. Genius)

In ancient times they were simply spirits. Later the term was changed to jinn in Muslim lore. In modern times there have been many stories about genies in bottles granting wishes, usually in some form of Arabic legend.

God of Forces:

The god that the Antichrist will worship, recorded in Daniel 11:38. This is probably connected with ancestor worship as was the pre-flood religion. Some modern translations have "god of fortresses" instead of "god of forces."

Ghost:

A ghost is supposed to be the spirit of a human who has died. Scripture states Christians are "with the Lord" after death (2 Corinthians 5:8). The disciples thought Jesus was a ghost (Greek: phantasm) when He came to them walking on the water (Matthew 14:26; Mark 6:49).

Giants:

1) Pre-flood children of the "sons of God" and the "daughters of men" (Genesis 6:1-6).
2) In the post-flood world we see giants in the land of Canaan. Og, the king of Bashan, was close to thirteen feet in height (Deut. 3:11). Amos 2:9 states some Amorites were as tall as cedar trees.

Gibborim: (mighty ones)

Another name for the Nephilim mentioned in Genesis 6.

God of Forces:

The god created and worshiped by the Antichrist (Daniel 11:38). Some have theorized it is a proper name; the god Maozim. Translated into English, the word means either a god of fortresses or a god of forces. In context with Daniel and Revelation, I believe it should be translated god of forces. The Antichrist will reincorporate the pre-flood religious idea of ancestor worship.

God of this World:
A title Paul used for Satan in 2 Corinthians 4:4.

Gog:
Gog is the king over Meshech and Tubal (Russia) that will attack Israel in the last days, according to Ezekiel 38-39. The basis for the belief that Magog is Russia stems from the *Book of Jasher* which states the descendants of Magog were called the Scythians. In Amos 7:1 LXX, Gog is called the king of the locusts. This suggests that Gog might be the demonic King of the Locusts described in Revelation 9. In a Targum (commentary on Numbers 11:26) it is stated that "Eldad and Medad prophesied that in the end of the days, Gog and Magog will come up against Jerusalem with their army and will fall by the hand of the king Messiah."

Golden Calf:
See Calf.

Guardian Angels:
Angels assigned to individuals to protect and guide them. Jesus mentioned them in Matthew 18:10. One of the earliest references to them is in the *Book of Jubilees* 35:17.

Fallen Angels

H

Hairy Ones: (Hebrew: Seirim)
Called devils or goat demons in some translations, these
demonic spirits are mentioned in Leviticus 17:7.
Jeroboam created high places for their worship in 2
Chronicles 11:15.

Hades:
One of two words translated hell in the New Testament.
The other is Gehenna. Hades is the Greek word for the
Hebrew word sheol, meaning the abode of the dead,
while Gehenna is the word for the lake of fire.

Hahya:
One of the sons of the fallen angel Semyaza.

Hanhel:
In rabbinic lore, the name of the angel who instructed
Balaam to build the seven altars, recorded in Numbers
22-23.

Heaven:
The place where God dwells.

Helel:
The Hebrew name for Lucifer found in Isaiah 14:12.
Interestingly, Canaanite mythology also states it was
Helel who tried to usurp the throne of Almighty God
and was cast down to the abyss.

Hell:

Hell in the Old Testament refers to the place where the dead (both good and bad) are kept. Paul states in 2 Corinthians 5:8 that saints dwell with God in heaven now. The New Testament concept of hell (Hades in Greek) is a place where the wicked dead are held until judgment, at which time the wicked will be thrown into the lake of fire (Gehenna).

Hermes:

Greek god of flocks and reincarnation. In Acts 14:12 Paul and Barnabas were witnessing to the heathen who tried to worship them, calling Barnabas Zeus because he was doing most of the talking; and Paul they called the god Hermes.

Hermon, Mt.:

According to the *Book of Enoch*, Mount Hermon is where the two hundred angels descended in the days of Jared. It is located in northern Israel close to Syria and Lebanon.

Holy Spirit:

The Comforter of John 14:26 and the third person of the Trinity.

Hubal:

Pre-Islamic Arabian deity connected with divination. The idol of Hubal is that of a human with a golden right hand. Many connect Hubal with the moon god Allah.

Hurmiz:

According to the Talmud she is one of the daughters of Lillith.

Fallen Angels

ℐ

Iblis:
An alternate spelling of Eblis

Idol:
A three-dimensional image of a being venerated or worshiped. Any such image is forbidden by the second of the Ten Commandments found in Exodus 20:4-5. In 1 Corinthians 5:11, Paul teaches sincere Christians are not to associate with people who call themselves Christians and practice idolatry.

Iim: (Iyim)
In Isaiah 13:22; 34:14; and Jeremiah 50:39 Iim are seen as demonic creatures who meet with the seirim and the siyim in the desolate places. This word is sometimes translated as jackals or wild beasts.

Incubi: (sing. incubus)
Male demons who come in the night to have sex with women. The opposite of a succubus. Ancient church fathers Justin Martyr, Tertullian, and Clement taught this was a misunderstanding based on the story of the sons of God (fallen angels) in Genesis 6.

Inias:
One of the seven angels reprobated by the church of Rome in AD 745. See *Uriel.*

Fallen Angels

Irin: (Hebrew, Irin qaddisim, holy watchers)
A class of angel seen in Daniel 4:17. See *watchers*.

Ischim: (Aishim, Izachim, Ishim, Issim)
An order of angels, compare to Psalm 104:4. In *Legends of the Jews* they are said to be composed of snow and fire.

Ishtar:
A Mesopotamian goddess of love, war, and the planet Venus. Other names for her are Inanna and Astarte, and she is connected with the ritual of weeping for Tammuz.

𝒥

Jael:
One of the Cherubim on the mercy seat. The other was Zarall.

Jesus: (Hebrew: Yeshua)
The name of the Messiah, second person of the Trinity. He is not an angel. Isaiah 12:2-3 hints that the Messiah's name would be Yeshua, Jesus. See *Ancient Prophecies Revealed.*

Jezebel:
Priestess of the Baal cult in 1 Kings 16-21. Rituals for Baal included the priests cutting themselves and frantic dancing. Revelation 2:18-29 reveals the Jezebel spirit influences people to partake of food used in ritual sacrifice to idols and to commit fornication.

Jinn:
According to Muslim theology Jinn are spirits between angels and man. They were created two thousand years before Adam. The modern genie in a bottle is based on this myth.

Jupiter: (Zeus)
In Acts 14:12, the people of Lystra thought Barnabas was Jupiter (king of the Greek gods). When the first century church sought to convert many to Christianity, they found Roman historical records that proved the Greco-

Roman gods were mere mortals who had died. They even disclosed where they were buried! They were never gods at all. See *Ancient Prost-flood History* for details.

Kaiwan:

According to Amos 5:25-27, Kaiwan was a demon worshiped by some Israelites in the wilderness. In Acts 7:43 he is called Remphan. Most believe this is the equivalent of the Greek god Saturn.

Kal:

The guardian angel of Nebuchadnezzar according to *Legends of the Jews*.

Fallen Angels

L

Lake of fire:
The final destination of evil humans, angels, and demons. They will be judged and thrown into the lake of fire according to Revelation 20:10, 13-15.

Legion:
The demonic name given by the possessed man in Mark 5:9, 15. Jesus cast out the demons and they went into a herd of pigs that immediately drowned themselves.

Leviathan:
Job 41:1; Isaiah 27:1; Revelation 12:9. In many of the Near East cultures it was a seven-headed, red dragon-like creature who represented an incredible evil to manifest in the end times. We see the seven-headed, red dragon in Revelation 13 and 17.

Lillith:
Translated "screech owl" in Isaiah 34:14, Lillith was a night demoness who preyed on children, according to the Talmud. There may be a connection between Lillith and Ishtar / Asharah worshipped by some ancient Israelites. She is sometimes depicted as having horns and four wings, like cherubim. She is usually seen on coins riding a beast, usually a lion. On rock formations she is seen having bird talons instead of feet.

Living Creatures:

Four creatures who guard the throne of God in Revelation 4:8. They each have six wings and many eyes within and without. One has the face of a lion, one of a calf, one of a man, and one of a flying eagle.

Lucifer:

Lucifer is the Latin name for Satan given in Isaiah 14:12. Some translations have it as "day star." The Hebrew name given there is Helel. Helel (Satan) was an anointed Cherub who fell through pride. See the chapter on *Lucifer's Rebellion*.

Lying Spirit:

In 1 Kings 22:22 God allowed a spirit to send a false dream / vision to all the false prophets to cause an evil king to go to war. Thinking he would be victorious, the king was killed. All true Bible-believing Christians who continually study the Word of God will never be fooled by such a lying spirit, just like Micaiah, the only true prophet in this passage, was not fooled.

Mahwey:
The son of the fallen angel Barakel, according to Enoch.

Malcolm:
Alternate name for Molech

Manah:
Goddess / angel of fertility worshiped in ancient Arabia. Her idol in the kabbah was destroyed on orders from Mohammud. Manah may be same as Manat, one of the daughters of the moon god Allah. See *Qur'an, surah 53.*

Manna: (Hebrew, What is this?)
The food of the angels. It is mentioned in Psalm 78:24, 25. The children of Israel ate it during their forty years in the wilderness. Elijah ate it twice — and didn't need to eat again for forty days (1 Kings 19:5-8)!

Man of Macedonia:
The angel who appeared to Paul in Acts 16:9-10 telling him to go to Macedonia to preach the gospel.

Marduk:
A god worshiped in ancient Babylon. According to Jasher, Mardon was the son of Nimrod who was later deified as the god Marduk. This shows one of the many instances of gods and goddesses being simply deified kings and queens.

Fallen Angels

Manat:

Manat was one of the crane angels / goddesses in ancient
pagan Arabia prayed to for intercession. Al Lat, Al
Ussa, and Manat were the three daughters of the
Arabian moon god. The three daughters are mentioned
in the Quran, surah 53.

Many-Eyed Ones:

A class of angel mentioned in Ezekiel 10:20 that the
rabbis call ofanim or "many-eyed ones." The living
creatures of Revelation have many eyes "within and
without."

Marian Apparitions:

A spirit claiming to be the Virgin Mary appears to
Catholics from time to time. She states she is the "queen
of heaven" and all grace comes though her, not Jesus
Christ. We are warned about such demonic imposters in
passages like Galatians 1:8-9 and 2 Corinthians 11:3-4,
13-14.

Mastema:

The name for Satan in the *Book of Jubilees*, Zadokite
Fragments, and other Dead Sea Scrolls.

Mercury: (Greek: Hermes)

One of the gods worshiped by the Greeks and Romans. In
Acts 14:11-12, the people at Lystra thought Paul was
Mercury come down to them because of the miracles
Paul and Barnabas performed. This allowed them to
effectively preach the gospel.

Messiah:
See Christ

Michael:
Michael disputed with Satan concerning the body of Moses in Jude 9. A Jewish legends states Michael wrote Psalm 85. He is called the "prince of light" in the Dead Sea Scroll *the Sons of Light vs. the Sons of Darkness.*

Midday Demon:
In Psalm 91:6 the word translated "destruction" is Qeteb. The rabbis teach that Qeteb is a demonic spirit that comes in the daytime and brings a plague, as opposed to the demon Deber, translated pestilence, in this passage. Reshpeh, the nighttime demon was well known to the Canaanites. The LXX of this verse says "the demon of midday."

Milcom:
Underworld fire deity of the Ammonites. He is sometimes connected to the god Nergal and was supposed to have been a rephaim. He may be the same as the biblical Molech, but this has not been completely proven.

Molech:
The Ammonite fire god worshiped by sacrificing children in the flames (Leviticus 18:21). Solomon built an altar to him in 1 Kings 11:7. The rabbis teach his temple was in the valley of Hinnom. In his temple there was a hollow statue with outstretched arms that would get so hot by the fire built inside it, they would glow. It was on

these outstretched, super heated arms whew infants and children would be placed for sacrifice.

Moroni:

The angel who supposedly gave revelations to Joseph Smith, founder of the Mormon cult.

N

Nammah:
1) the prophetess, daughter of Enoch, wife of Noah, mother of Ham, Shem, and Japheth.
2) daughter of Lamech, descendant of Cain, wife of the fallen angel Azazel and/or Semyaza and mother of the Sedim.

Nasarach:
An alternate spelling of the Assyrian god Nisroch found in Isaiah and 2 Kings 19:37.

Necromancer:
The Canaanite form of sorcery where the practitioner would lie on a grave after performing a ritual and go to sleep to communicate with the deceased in his dreams. It is a forbidden practice listed in Deuteronomy 18:11. Necromancers were also called dreamers by the ancient rabbis. See also *Wizard* and *Divination*.

Nehushtan: (Hebrew: thing of brass)
In 2 Kings 18:4, the name given by King Hezekiah to the brass serpent Moses made in the wilderness (Numbers 21:8-9). Some thought a residue of the power to heal might be still in it. When Hezekiah realized the Israelites made it into an idol of veneration / relic, he had it destroyed.

Fallen Angels

Nephilim:
Originally the children of the sons of God and daughters of men mentioned in Genesis 6. In post-flood days groups of people with some genetic tampering were classified as a type of Nephilim. These were the Emim, Rephaim, Gibborim, Zamzummim, and others.

Nergal: (great hero, king of death)
The god of Cuth in 2 Kings 17:30. May be the same as Molech.

Nisroch: (the great eagle)
An Assyrian god worshiped by Sennacherib in 2 Kings 19:37. He has been compared to the false gods Chemos, Baal-Peor, Meserach, and Arasek.

Nego: (Nego, Nebo)
In Babylonian mythology, the angel who records one's deeds and hands them over to the angel of death when it is time for one to die. In Daniel 1:6-7 Azariah was renamed Abednego, meaning servant of Nego or Nebo.

Nimrod:
Nimrod sought to recreate the false religion of the pre-flood world. According to the *Ancient Book of Jasher 11*, Nimrod created temples for the observance of the stars. He commanded his subjects to worship each of the twelve signs of the Zodiac in their order. His son, Mardon, was killed in battle and was later deified as the Babylonian god Marduk.

O

Ophannim: (wheels)
The rabbinical name for the "many-eyed ones."

Og:
The giant king of Bashan whose bed was thirteen and a half feet long by six feet wide (Deuteronomy 3:11). He was killed by Moses, in Numbers 21:33-35, and was the last of the Rephaim.

Ohya:
One of the sons of the fallen angel Semyaza.

Oribel:
A variant spelling of Uriel, one of the angels reprobated by Pope Zachary in AD 745. See *Reprobated Angels*.

Osiris:
One of the ancient Egyptian gods. The *Ancient Book of Jasher 14:2* records he was originally a first dynasty king of Egypt, later worshiped as a god.

Ou:
A variant of Uriel found in the Dead Sea Scroll called *The War of the Sons of Light Against the Sons of Darkness*.

Ouranos:
A variant of Uranus or heaven. Even though he was worshiped as a god in the Greco-Roman world, he was

one of the princes who ruled in the early post-flood world. Zeus and Hercules were two other deified kings of that period, according to the ancient church fathers.

Overshadowing Cherub:
The title for Satan given in Ezekiel 28:16.

Penual:
An angel who wrestled with Jacob at Peniel in Genesis 32:30.

Phadihel:
Jewish legend gives this name to the angel who came to Manoah's wife (mother of Samson).

Phanuel:
An angel mentioned in *4 Ezra* and the *Sybille Oracles*.

Prince of Persia:
An angel / demon who withstood Gabriel and Michael in Daniel 10:13. See *Dubbiel.*

Prince of Grecia:
An angel / demon of Greece who was to take over control after the prince of Persia was defeated in Daniel 10:13.

Prince of the Power of the Air:
The title for Satan given by Paul in Ephesians 2:2.

Prince, Chief:
A term for spiritual rulers over nations found in Daniel 10:13.

The Priestesses of Asharah

In Jeremiah 7:18, 44:18-19, 25, Israelite women made crescent moon-shaped cakes and dedicated them to Asharah. In this festival she was known as the "Queen of Heaven." We are also told no men could be present at this festival. Augustine (*De civit dei 2.3*) says orgies were a part of her worship and some of her priests were eunuchs in women's clothes.

Ezekiel 13:17-21 says the daughters of Israel fastened "magic bands" (kesatot) to their wrists and with them "trapped souls like birds." This word, *kesatot*, occurs only once in the Old Testament. It is related to the Sumerian KI-ShU, meaning a kind of magical imprisonment. It is also related to the Greek word, κιστε, which is a small vial, used in certain mystery rituals of the Dionysian cult. The symbol of the κιστε on Dionysian pictograms is a basket with a snake emerging.

If they actually had magical (sorcery) vials that were symbolized by a venomous serpent and trapped people into doing what they wanted, I believe that Ezekiel was telling us the Asharah priestesses used a very addictive drug to enslave their worshipers. The ingredients of this drug are currently unknown.

Prince of this World:
The title for Satan given by Jesus in John 12:31.

Possession:

Possession takes place when a disembodied spirit attaches itself to a human being, controlling the person's behavior and thoughts. The demon doing this can be banished through what is called an exorcism.

Pythoness:

Acts 16:16 records that the apostle Paul cast a spirit out of a girl who divined the future. The word for "divination" in the KJV is "Pythoness" in Greek. A pythoness was a Delphic oracle who used drugs and meditation (like T.M. and contemplative prayer) to create a state of ecstasy whereby she would become possessed by a spirit.

Fallen Angels

Q

Qeteb:
Appearing rarely in the Old Testament (Deuteronomy 32:24; Ps. 91:5-6) usually translated as "pestilence" or "plague" was a well known demon among the Semitic peoples. See *Midday Demon*.

Queen of Angels:
A tile given by Catholics to the Virgin Mary.

Queen of Heaven:
An ancient goddess mentioned in Jeremiah 7:18; 44:17-19, 25. She may have been connected with Ishtar, Astarte, and Venus. Jeremiah 44:19 indicates part of her ritual was for women only, no men could be present. In modern times a spirit calling itself "Mary" has appeared to numerous Catholics. She referred to herself as the queen of heaven and the queen of the angels. She also teaches co-redemptrix theology, namely that she has the power to grant grace and forgiveness in the place of Jesus Christ and the Father. These are considered demonic doctrines among Protestants and the Eastern Orthodox.

Fallen Angels

Raguel:
One of the angels reprobated by Rome in AD 745. See *Uriel*.

Rahab:
Mentioned in Isaiah 51:9, Job 26:13, and Psalm 87:4; 89:10 as another name for *Leviathan*.

Rahmiel:
Roman Catholic legend states Saint Francis of Assisi was transformed into the angel Rahmiel upon his death. Biblically we know people do not transform into angels any more than they evolve into cats after death.

Ramiel:
An angel mentioned in the *Book of Enoch* and in the *Sibylline Oracles*.

Raphael: (God has healed)
He appears as a healing angel in the apocryphal book of *Tobit*. He is called a watcher in the *Book of Enoch*. Some ancient church fathers credit the miracle of the healing water mentioned in John 5:4 with Raphael. See *Angel Who Troubled the Water*.

Raziel:
A fictitious angel who supposedly wrote the medieval grimoire called the *Book of the Angel Raziel*.

Fallen Angels

Remiel:
An alternate spelling for Ramiel

Remphan:
A star god that the Israelites worshiped in the wilderness
mentioned in Acts 7:43. Stephan's quote was from
Amos 5:25-27 where the Hebrew name for Remphan
was Chiun. Remphan is probably connected with the
Greek god Saturn.

Rephaim:
In the Bible the Rephaim are post-flood giants who were
very anti-God. Ugaritic texts (Canaanite) describe the
Rephaim as ancestors who may grant them immortal
life by ascending to godhood. They are prayed to for the
blessing of crops and a seven-day banquet is held in
their honor.

Reprobated Angels:
Pope Zachary called a church council in Rome. The
Lateran Council was held on October 25, AD 745.
Bishops Clement and Adalbert were convicted of the
heresy of veneration of seven angels for the purpose of
healing, divination, and other occult practices. These
seven angels were Uriel, Raguel, Inais, Adamus,
Semibel, Tubuael, and Sabaothe. After this, the Roman
Catholic Church only allowed the veneration of the
angles Michael, Gabriel, and Raphael.

Resep:

Known as Resheph in Akkad and Ebla, the word rarely appears in the Hebrew Old Testament, usually along with the demon Qeteb. See *Midday Demon*.

Rimmon:

A thunder god / demon worshiped in Damascus, Syria. He is mentioned in 2 Kings 5:18.

Fallen Angels

S

Sacaoc:
One of the seven angels reprobated in AD 745. See *Reprobated Angels*.

Sakkuth:
Another name for Kaiwan / Saturn found in some Babylonians texts. It may be mentioned in Amos 5:26 as "tabernacle."

Samael: (poison god)
A fallen angel named in the Talmud.

Sar: (prince, pl. sarim)
A term sometimes referring to angels. The rabbis stated there were seventy sarim over the seventy nations.

Sariel:
A warrior angel named in the Dead Sea Scroll entitled *The War of the Sons of Light Against the Sons of Darkness*.

Sarim: (shining ones)
Psalm 82:7 refers to those who think of themselves as gods. They will die like men or fall like the Sarim (princes). Sarim is a Hebrew word that can mean princes or a fallen angelic / demonic creatures.

Fallen Angels

Satan: (the adversary)

Satan, Lucifer, is the leader of the fallen angels. His Hebrew name, Helel, is translated Lucifer in Isaiah 14:12 KJV. We also learn from Isaiah 14:13-15 that Satan wanted to usurp God's throne and was expelled from heaven. Ezekiel 28:14 shows that he is a fallen *cherub*. Job 1:6-7 records that he comes before God along with other fallen angels to accuse the saints. Jesus mentioned in Luke 10:18 that He personally witnessed Satan's fall. We see him in the Garden of Eden in the form of a serpent tempting Eve and causing the fall of mankind. Revelation 20:1-10 records that he will be bound for one thousand years, then released to tempt the nations one last time before being thrown into the lake of fire for all eternity.

Saturn:

The Roman name for the Greek god Cronus. He was originally a post-flood king who ruled in the area of Greece and was deified after his death (see *Ancient Post-Flood History*). He is connected with the god Chiun (Amos 5:26) who was also called Remphan in Acts 7:43.

Satyrs: (Hebrew: Seirim)
See *Seirim*

Screech Owl:

The term found in Isaiah 34:14 KJV for the demoness Lillith.

Sedim:

The descendants of the angels Azael and/or Semyaza and the evil Nammah, daughter of Lemech, before the Flood, according to Jewish legend. After the Flood the Sedim were venerated by the Assyrians as guardian spirits. In the Talmud they are said to be spirits invoked for the purpose of exorcism. This might be what Jesus was referring to when he asked the Jews by whom did they cast out demons in Matthew 12:27.

Seirim: (Hebrew: hairy ones)

Called Satyrs or goat demons in some modern Bibles. In 2 Chronicles 11:15 they are translated "devils." This verse records that Jeroboam created a cult with priests and high places for their worship. They are not described, but are also mentioned in Isaiah 13:21; 34:14.

Semyaza: (Shemyaza, Azza)

One of the leaders of the two hundred angels of the second rebellion. His two greatest sons were Hahya and Ohya.

Seraphim: (sing. Seraph, fiery)

A class of angels who have six wings (three pairs) and are fiery-like in appearance. The rabbis said their true form was serpent-like. The Hebrew word "seraph" is used in Isaiah 6:2 to refer to this class of angel and in Numbers 21:6 to refer to fiery serpents found in the wilderness.

Fallen Angels

Serpent:

Genesis 3 records how Satan appeared in the form of a talking serpent to temp Eve and cause the fall of mankind. The serpent and the dragon have always been metaphors for Satan.

Shasta:

The Shasta is an ancient document that shows the major gods worshiped by the Hindus were originally the angels who fell, and proves that before the Hindu corruption, they worshiped one true god, as all ancient post-flood people did. The Shasta was mentioned as proof of Christianity's truth by the USA's founding fathers, John Adams, Ben Franklin, and others.

Shedu:

Babylonian name for the Sedim. They were "guardian spirits" venerated in Babylon and invoked in similar fashion as the Assyrian and Hebrew spirits in exorcism rites. See *Sedim*.

Shemesh:

Another Canaanite sun god deity.

Sheol:

The Hebrew word for the place where the spirits of dead humans are kept. The Greek word for this is Hades. It is not the same as the lake of fire or Tartarus.

Simon Magus:

A man who tried to buy the Holy Spirit from Peter. See Acts 8:9. He later became very evil and history records him as the father of the Gnostic cults.

Son of God, the:

A title for Jesus Christ used throughout the Old and New Testaments, 2 Esdras 1611 KJV, the *Book of Enoch*, and other Dead Sea Scrolls.

Sons of God:

While Christians are referred to as adopted "sons of God," the term usually refers to being created directly by God. Hence, both Adam and the angels are called sons of God. Angels are referred to as sons of God in passages like Genesis 6:4; Job 1:6; 38:7; etc.

Sorcery:

The use of meditation (Like T.M. or contemplative prayer) and rituals to communicate with spirits or see visions. Modern examples of these include tarot cards, Ouija boards, astrology, and the like. Occult tools and sorcery / meditation are forbidden in Deuteronomy 18:10-11.

Sparks:

An alternate term referring to the Tarshishim, a class of angels. They are also called "brilliant ones" and "splendors."

Fallen Angels

Splendors:
Another name for the Tarshishim.

Succubi: (sing. succubus)
Female demons that come in the night to have sex with
men. The opposite of a incubus. Ancient church fathers
Justin Martyr, Tertullian, and Clement taught this was a
misunderstanding based on the story of the sons of God
(fallen angels) in Genesis 6. Although angels are all
male, the spirits of their children (demons) could be
either male or female.

Tarshishim: (brilliant ones)
A class of angel, according to the rabbis. Also called sparks, splendors.

Tarsisim:
Another name for the Tarshishim.

Tartarus:
Tartarus is translated hell in 2 Peter 2:4. Enoch 22 records there were three compartments in the underworld: one for the evil dead, one for the saints (Luke 16:22 calls this Abraham's bosom), and one for the fallen angels from Azazel's Rebellion. During the Great Tribulation, those fallen angels will be released as locusts from the bottomless pit (Revelation 9:1-11).

Tarot Deck:
A deck of cards originating from the thirteenth century used for fortune telling.

Talisman:
A piece of jewelry that is supposed to bring good luck to the wearer by its magic power.

Tammuz:
Tammuz was a sun god whose death on December 22 was mourned annually by women. His worship was recorded in Ezekiel 8:14. Tammuz was connected with the

worship of the Queen of Heaven in Jeremiah 7:18; 44:17-19, 25.

Theophany:

A Christophany, or pre-incarnate appearance of Christ

Thummim:

See Urim.

Teraphim:

Teraphim are mentioned in Genesis 31:19, 34; Hosea 3:4; Matthew 24:15; and Revelation 13:15. Idols do not speak or do anything at all, according to the Bible, but teraphim do. The Antichrist creates one that both speaks and causes those who do not take the mark of the beast to be killed. The only description we have of teraphim comes from the *Book of Jasher*.

"[40]And Rachel stole her father's images, and she took them and she concealed them upon the camel upon which she sat, and she went on. [41]And this is the manner of the images; in taking a man who is the first born and slaying him and taking the hair off his head, and taking salt and salting the head and anointing it in oil, then taking a small tablet of copper or a tablet of gold and writing the name upon it, and placing the tablet under his tongue, and taking the head with the tablet under the tongue and putting it in the house, and lighting up lights before it and bowing down to it. [42]And at the time when they bow down to it, it speaketh to them in all matters that they ask of it, through the power of the name which is written in it. [43]And some make them in the figures of men, of gold and silver, and go to them in times known to them, and the figures receive the influence of the stars, and tell them future things, and in this manner were the images which Rachel stole from her father. *Ancient Book of Jasher 31:40-43*

Trinity:

The Bible teaches there is only one God, who manifested in three Persons. This is called the Trinity. Those who say there are three separate and distinct gods are tritheists and those who deny the divinity of Jesus would be strict monotheists or henotheists. Jesus said in John 8:24, "If ye believe not that 'I AM' ye shall die in your sins." This is why Trinitarian denominations are considered true Christians and non-Trinitarian denomination are considered cults.

Fallen Angels

Ｕ

Unclean Spirit:
An evil demonic spirit connected with ritual impurity. We see unclean spirits once in the Old Testament (Zechariah 13:2) and twenty-one times in the New Testament. They possess men (Matthew 12:43); they know God, Jesus, and the prophecies (Mark 1:23); they can give supernatural strength and cause people to cut themselves (Mark 5:2-5); they are under the control of Satan (Mark 7:25-26; Luke 4:33); and cause disease (Luke 9:42).

Uriel: (light of God, fire of God)
The *Book of Enoch* 10:1-3 states it was Uriel who warned Noah about the coming flood. The *midrash Aggada Exodus*, a rabbinical commentary on Exodus, states it was Uriel who came to kill Moses when he refused to circumcise Gershom. He relented when Zipporah did the rite for him. He is also mentioned in 2 Esdras. In the Middle Ages he was used as a focal point for astrology and angelic magic in occult books. This caused a council to excommunicate anyone who invoked Uriel or other angels for magical purposes. See *Reprobate Angels*.

Urim and Thummim: (light and perfection / truth)
Two sardonyx crystals on the top part of the High Priest's breastplate used to divine God's will for the people (Exodus 28:30; Leviticus 8:8). Josephus, in his

Antiquities of the Jews 3, records that when God was present the Urim would glow. Then, and only then, could the high priest ask questions. The Thummim would glow in answer to a yes or no question. On other occasions when a question of which tribe would go up to battle was asked, the crystal in the breastplate that represented that tribe would glow. The Talmud, *Yoma*, states they were one of five holy objects from the first temple that were missing from the second temple.

Uziel: (Usiel, Uzziel, strength of God)
One of the fallen angels who sinned in Genesis 6 according to the *Tagum of Onkeles ben Johnathan*, on Genesis 6:4.

Valiant Ones: (Arelim, Erelim)
A class of angel sometimes described as white fire. The Hebrew word is translated as valiant ones in Isaiah 33:7 KJV.

Victor:
The angel who told St. Patrick to return to Ireland and convert the pagans.

Virtues:
A class of angels in Rabbinic lore equated with the Tarshishim. Church father Eusebius says of Christ, "The Virtues of Heaven, seeing Him rise, surrounded Him to form His escort." This may mean the ancient church considered the two angels at Christ's tomb to be of the order of Virtues.

Vishna: a mighty angel mentioned in the Hindu text *Bhagavad Gita*. See *Shasta*.

Vishnu: according to the *Bhagavad Gita*
Vishnu is the supreme God / avatar who sustains the universe. Brahma was the creator and Shiva will be its destroyer. See *Shasta*.

Fallen Angels

W

Watcher: (Hebrew, Irin qaddisim, holy watchers)
A class of angel mentioned in Daniel 4:13. The rabbis said these angels never sleep and were appointed to watch over men. Many other texts like 2 Esdras, Enoch, Jubilees, and other Dead Sea Scrolls tell how some of the watchers fell into sin with the daughters of men. Genesis 6 does not call them watchers, but does tell their story.

Wheels: (many-eyed ones)
A class of angel called "ofanim" by Talmudists.

Wild Beasts: (Hebrew: Siyyim)
Demonic spirits mentioned in Isaiah 13:21; 34:14; and Jeremiah 50:39. These dwell in the dry land. Jesus mentions when demons are cast out of a man they don't like the dry places, so they return to repossess the man (Matthew 12:43). This might be a reference to these beings.

Wizard: (Hebrew: Yidde'oni)
The practices of the Canaanite wizard is forbidden in Deuteronomy 18:10. The Talmud states that the name for a wizard, Yidde'oni, comes from a word loosely translated as an extinct animal. It also states that no one remembers exactly what kind of animal it was. The name was carried over to mean those who used a bone of this extinct animal by placing it in their mouths and

through some incantations could have the dead speak through this bone. This has been translated as a ventriloquist or a medium. It is quite possible that the term in this ancient passage means, instead of "extinct animal," a bone from the deceased. Mediums today often ask for an artifact of the deceased in order to try to make some sort of contact with them. See also *Divination* and *Necromancer*.

World Rulers:

The Greek words "Kosmokratoros skotos" in Ephesians 6:12 literally means "beings of darkness who rule the world." This gives us the understanding that in certain ways fallen angels / demons control many aspects of this fallen world.

Wormwood:

In Revelation 8:11, a star called wormwood falls from heaven and poisons one third of the water. This star is thought by some to be an angel or demon.

Yah:
Shortened form of Yahweh

Yahweh:
The Hebrew name for God. The Latin equivalent is Jehovah. Since the name of God is never to be taken as a curse word, the ancient rabbis opted to say the word Adonai (Lord) when they saw God's name written. Over the centuries the proper pronunciation of the name was nearly forgotten. In the KJV when you see the word Lord, it is Adonai in Hebrew, but when you see LORD (all caps), it is the name of God, Yahweh.

Fallen Angels

Ȝ

Zamzummim:

A tribe of Rephaim who were the former inhabitants of the land then occupied by the Ammonites. They are recorded in Deuteronomy 2:20. In other Hebrew texts they seem to be connected with evil spirits. They may therefore be the evil spirits of the Nephilim who were destroyed before the flood. The area of Ammon, Jordan, was their original home. Archeology should find evidence of their existence near Ammon.

Zarall:

One of the cherubs on the mercy seat. The other was Jael.

Zeus:

The chief god of the Greeks. In Acts 14:12 the heathen of Lystra thought Barnabas was Zeus (Jupiter) come down to them. It gave him an opportunity to preach the gospel to them.

Ziim:

The Ziim are translated "wild beasts" in Isaiah 13:21 and Jeremiah 50:39. They are translated "them that dwell in the wilderness" in Isaiah 23:13. Not much is known about these demonic creatures.

Zodiac:

The zodiac is a collection of twelve constellations that the sun, moon, and planets move through. They were originally connected with the ancient pre-flood paganism that caused the destruction of earth in Noah's Flood. Nimrod was one of the first post-flood kings to try to bring back the concept of ancestor worship and added the worship of the twelve constellations as gods.

"Terah brought Abram into the chamber of the inner court, and Abram saw, and behold the whole room was full of gods of wood and stone, twelve great images and others less than they without number." *Ancient book of Jasher 11:20*

Other Books by Ken Johnson, Th.D.

Ancient Post-Flood History
Historical Documents That Point to a Biblical Creation.

This book is a Christian timeline of ancient post-Flood history based on Bible chronology, the early church fathers, and ancient Jewish and secular history. This can be used as a companion guide in the study of Creation Science.

Some questions answered: Who were the Pharaohs in the times of Joseph and Moses? When did the famine of Joseph occur? What Egyptian documents mention these? When did the Exodus take place? When did the Kings of Egypt start being called "Pharaoh" and why?

Who was the first king of a united Italy? Who was Zeus and where is he buried? Where did Shem and Ham rule and where are they buried?

How large was Nimrod's invasion force that set up the Babylonian Empire, and when did this invasion occur? What is Nimrod's name in Persian documents?

How can we use this information to witness to unbelievers?

Ancient Seder Olam
A Christian Translation of the 2000-year-old Scroll

This 2000-year-old scroll reveals the chronology from Creation through Cyrus' decree that freed the Jews in 536 BC. The *Ancient Seder Olam* uses biblical prophecy to prove its calculations of the timeline. We have used this technique to continue the timeline all the way to the reestablishment of the nation of Israel in AD 1948.

Using the Bible and rabbinical tradition, this book shows that the ancient Jews awaited King Messiah to fulfill the prophecy spoken of in Daniel, Chapter 9. The Seder answers many questions about the chronology of the books of Kings and Chronicles. It talks about the coming of Elijah, King Messiah's reign, and the battle of Gog and Magog.

This scroll and the Jasher scroll are the two main sources used in Ken's first book, *Ancient Post-Flood History*.

Ancient Prophecies Revealed
500 Prophecies Listed In Order Of When They Were Fulfilled

This book details over 500 biblical prophecies in the order they were fulfilled; these include pre-flood times though the First Coming of Jesus and into the Middle Ages. The heart of this book is the 53 prophecies fulfilled between 1948 and 2008. The last 11 prophecies between 2008 and the Tribulation are also given. All these are documented and interpreted from the Ancient Church Fathers.

The Ancient Church Fathers, including disciples of the twelve apostles, were firmly premillennial, pretribulational, and very pro-Israel.

Ancient Book of Jasher
Referenced in Joshua 10:13; 2 Samuel 1:18; 2 Timothy 3:8

There are thirteen ancient history books mentioned and recommended by the Bible. The Ancient Book of Jasher is the only one of the thirteen that still exists. It is referenced in Joshua 10:13; 2 Samuel 1:18; and 2 Timothy 3:8. This volume contains the entire ninety-one chapters plus a detailed analysis of the supposed discrepancies, cross-referenced historical accounts, and detailed charts for ease of use. As with any history book, there are typographical errors in the text but with three consecutive timelines running though the histories, it is very easy to arrive at the exact dates of recorded events. It is not surprising that this ancient document confirms the Scripture and the chronology given in the Hebrew version of the Old Testament, once and for all settling the chronology differences between the Hebrew Old Testament and the Greek Septuagint.

Third Corinthians
Ancient Gnostics and the End of the World

This little known, 2000-year-old Greek manuscript was used in the first two centuries to combat Gnostic cults. Whether or not it is an authentic copy of the original epistle written by the apostle Paul, it gives an incredible look into the cults that will arise in the Last Days. It contains a prophecy that the same heresies that pervaded the first century church would return before the Second Coming of the Messiah.

Ancient Paganism
The Sorcery of the Fallen Angels

Ancient Paganism explores the false religion of the ancient pre-Flood world and its spread into the Gentile nations after Noah's Flood. Quotes from the ancient church fathers, rabbis, and the Talmud detail the activities and beliefs of both Canaanite and New Testament era sorcery. This book explores how, according to biblical prophecy, this same sorcery will return before the Second Coming of Jesus Christ to earth. These religious beliefs and practices will invade the end time church and become the basis for the religion of the Antichrist. Wicca, Druidism, Halloween, Yule, meditation, and occultic tools are discussed at length.

The Rapture
The Pretribulational Rapture of the Church Viewed From the Bible and the Ancient Church

This book presents the doctrine of the pretribulational Rapture of the church. Many prophecies are explored with Biblical passages and terms explained.

Evidence is presented that proves the first century church believed the End Times would begin with the return of Israel to her ancient homeland, followed by the Tribulation and the Second Coming. More than fifty prophecies have been fulfilled since Israel became a state.

Evidence is also given that several ancient rabbis and at least four ancient church fathers taught a pretribulational Rapture. This book also gives many of the answers to the arguments midtribulationists and posttribulationists use. It is our hope this book will be an indispensable guide for debating the doctrine of the Rapture.

Ancient Epistle of Barnabas
His Life and Teaching

The Epistle of Barnabas is often quoted by the ancient church fathers. Although not considered inspired Scripture, it was used to combat legalism in the first two centuries AD. Besides explaining why the Laws of Moses are not binding on Christians, the Epistle explains how many of the Old Testament rituals teach typological prophecy. Subjects explored are: Yom Kippur, the Red Heifer ritual, animal sacrifices, circumcision, the Sabbath, Daniel's visions and the end-time ten nation empire, and the temple.

The underlying theme is the Three-Fold Witness. Barnabas teaches that mature Christians must be able to lead people to the Lord, testify to others about Bible prophecy fulfilled in their lifetimes, and teach creation history and creation science to guard the faith against the false doctrine of evolution. This is one more ancient church document that proves the first century church was premillennial and constantly looking for the Rapture and other prophecies to be fulfilled.

The Ancient Church Fathers
What the Disciples of the Apostles Taught

This book reveals who the disciples of the twelve apostles were and what they taught, from their own writings. It documents the same doctrine was faithfully transmitted to their descendants in the first few centuries and where, when, and by whom, the doctrines began to change. The ancient church fathers make it very easy to know for sure what the complete teachings of Jesus and the twelve apostles were.

You will learn, from their own writings, what the first century disciples taught about the various doctrines that divide our church today. You will learn what was discussed at the seven general councils and why. You will learn who were the cults and cult leaders that began to change doctrine and spread their heresy and how that became to be the standard teaching in the medieval church. A partial list of doctrines discussed in this book are:

Abortion	Free will	Purgatory
Animal sacrifices	Gnostic cults	Psychology
Antichrist	Homosexuality	Reincarnation
Arminianism	Idolatry	Replacement theology
Bible or tradition	Islam	Roman Catholicism
Calvinism	Israel's return	The Sabbath
Circumcision	Jewish food laws	Salvation
Deity of Jesus Christ	Mary's virginity	Schism of Nepos
Demons	Mary's assumption	Sin / Salvation
Euthanasia	Meditation	The soul
Evolution	The Nicolaitans	Spiritual gifts
False gospels	Paganism	Transubstantiation
False prophets	Predestination	Yoga
Foreknowledge	Premillennialism	Women in ministry

Ancient Book of Daniel
The ancient Hebrew prophet Daniel lived in the fifth century BC and accurately predicted the history of the nation of Israel from 536 BC to AD 1948. He also predicted the date of the death of the Messiah to occur in AD 32, the date of the rebirth of the nation of Israel to occur in AD 1948, and the Israeli capture of the Temple Mount to take place in AD 1967! Commentary from the ancient rabbis and the first century church reveals how the messianic rabbis and the disciples of the apostles interpreted his prophecies.

Daniel also indicated where the Antichrist would come from, where he would place his international headquarters, and identified the three rebel nations that will attack him during the first three-and-a-half years of the Tribulation.

Ancient Epistles of John and Jude

This book provides commentary for the epistles of John and Jude from the ancient church fathers. It gives the history of the struggles of the first century church. You will learn which cults John and Jude were writing about and be able to clearly identify each heresy. You will also learn what meditation and sorcery truly are. At the end of each chapter is a chart contrasting the teaching of the church and that of the Gnostics. Included are master charts of the *doctrine of Christ*, the *commandments of Christ*, and the *teaching of the apostles*.

Learn the major doctrines that all Christians must believe:

Jesus is the only Christ	The Rapture
Jesus is the only Savior	Creationism
Jesus is the only begotten Son of God	Eternal life only by Jesus
Jesus is sinless	The sin nature
Jesus physically resurrected	Prophecy proves inspiration
Jesus will physically return to earth	Idolatry is evil
God is not evil	

Ancient Messianic Festivals, And The Prophecies They Reveal

The messianic festivals are the Biblical rituals God commanded the ancient Israelites to observe. These ancient rites give great detail on the first coming of the Messiah including the date on which He would arrive, the manner of His death, and the birth of His church. You will also learn of the many disasters that befell the Jews through the centuries on the ninth of Av. The rituals speak of a Natzal, or rapture of believers, and a terrible time called the *Yamin Noraim*. They give a rather complete outline of this seven-year tribulation period, including the rise of a false messiah. They also tell of a time when the earth will be at peace in the Messianic Kingdom. In addition to the seven messianic festivals, you will learn the prophetic outline of other ceremonies like Hanukkah, the new moon ceremony, the wedding ceremony, the ashes of the red heifer, and the ancient origins of

Halloween. You will also learn of other prophetical types and shadows mentioned in the Bible.

Ancient Word of God
Is there a verse missing from your Bible? Would you like to know why it was removed?

This book covers the history of the transmission of the Bible text through the centuries. It examines and proves, based on fulfilled Bible prophecy, which Greek texts faithfully preserve the ancient Word of God.

You will learn about the first century cults that created their own warped Bibles and of the warnings that the ancient church gave in regard to the pure text. Over two hundred English Bibles are compared. Is the KJV more accurate, maybe the NIV, or perhaps the NASB or ESV?

Cults and the Trinity
This book compares Christianity with the false religions of the world today based on the accuracy of fulfilled Bible prophecy. No other religion has used prophecy fulfilled in the reader's lifetime to prove its authority, except the Bible. With more than fifty prophecies fulfilled since AD 1948, and Jesus' teaching that He is the only way to salvation, we can conclude we must be a Christian to gain eternal life.

Jesus declares you must follow His teachings in order to obtain eternal life. Among these teachings is the fact that Jesus is God incarnate, the second person of the Trinity. Numerous church fathers' quotes dating back to the first century AD show this fact as well, and the ancient church defined a cult as a group claiming to be Christian but denying the Trinity.

Listing over one hundred cults and numerous subgroups, this book shows that virtually all of them are nontrinitarians. A detailed, yet simple, study on the Trinity will enable you to witness to all the cults using only this one doctrine.

Ancient Book of Enoch

The Holy Spirit inspired Jude to quote Enoch for a reason. The Ancient Book of Enoch opens by addressing those in the Tribulation period. It contains numerous prophecies about the flood and fire judgments, and the two comings of the Messiah. It teaches that the Messiah is the Son of God and that He will shed His blood to redeem us and even predicts the generation that this would occur!

The book of Enoch prophesies a window of time in which the Second Coming would occur and prophesies that there will be twenty-three Israeli Prime Ministers ruling in fifty-eight terms from AD 1948 to the beginning of the Tribulation period, and much more. Even though it prophesies that the Bible would be created and says we will be judged by our obedience to the Bible, it also makes it clear that this book is not to be added to the Canon of Scripture.

The Ancient Book of Enoch recounts the history of the angels who fell in the days of Jared, Enoch's father. It testifies to their marriages with human women and their genetic experiments. This commentary includes a previously unknown chapter from the Dead Sea Scrolls that actually explains how they did their genetic tampering.

Ancient Epistles of Timothy and Titus

This book provides commentary for the epistles of Timothy and Titus from the ancient church fathers. It describes the history of the struggles of the first century church. It reveals which heretics and cults Paul was writing about. It details the history of those heretics and their errors. Learn which Gnostic cults Alexander, Demas, Hymenaeus, Philetus, Phygellus, and Hermogenes were involved in, what heresies they taught, and exactly why Paul excommunicated them. At the end of each chapter is a chart contrasting the teaching of the church and that of the Gnostics. Included are master charts of *sound doctrine*, the *commandments of Christ*, and the *teaching of the apostles*.

For more information visit us at:

Biblefacts.org

Bibliography

Ken Johnson, *Ancient Prophecies Revealed*, Createspace, 2008

Ken Johnson, *Ancient Paganism*, Createspace, 2009

Ken Johnson, *Ancient Book of Jasher*, Createspace, 2008

Ken Johnson, *Ancient Book of Enoch*, Createspace, 2012

Eerdmans Publishing, *Ante-Nicene Fathers*, Eerdmans Publishing, 1886

Cruse, C. F, *Eusebius' Ecclesiastical History*, Hendrickson Publishers, 1998

David Bercot, *A Dictionary of Early Christian Beliefs*, Hendrickson Publishers, 1999

Ken Johnson, *Ancient Church Fathers*, Createspace, 2010

Louis Ginzberg, *Legends of the Jews*, Jewish Publication Society, 1954

E. M. Bounds, *Winning the Invisible War*, Whitaker House, 1984

Billy Graham, *Angels*, W. Publishing Group, 1994

Gustav Davidson, *Dictionary of Angels*, The Free Press, 1967

Made in the USA
Columbia, SC
12 January 2024

30362747R00078